Pillow Book of a Manic Depressive

Anthony Peck

chipmunkapublishing
the mental health publisher

Published by
Chipmunkapublishing
PO Box 6872
Brentwood
Essex CM13 1ZT
United Kingdom

http://www.chipmunkapublishing.com

Edited by Kirti Kaylan

Chipmunkapublishing gratefully acknowledge the support of Arts Council England.

A pillow book is an "informal [medieval Japanese] book of notes which men and women composed when they retired to their rooms in the evening and which they kept near their sleeping place, possibly in the drawers of their wooden pillows, so that they might record stray impressions."

Introduction to "The Pillow Book of Sei Shônagon", translated by Ivan Morris, 1967, Penguin Classics

Anthony Peck

Introduction

When I sat down to write this it was with no particular end in mind. I had just re-read Sei Shônagon's pillow book and wondered what a twenty-first century pillow book might be like. In fifteenth century aristocratic Japan the reflections were on court life, the changing seasons, personal intrigues, manners. Through Sei Shonagan's eyes and from her heart a picture is painted of her place and time that no regular history could capture. I thought it would be fun to see what a similar approach might reveal about today.

Besides, I had the time. I was recovering from a manic episode that had pretty much broken all of me. Plus I was coming to terms with my bi-polar diagnosis, receiving excellent treatment and guidance, and taking the time necessary to ensure a long happy life, with the ability to keep the beast under control.

Learning to adjust my thinking, and writing a book full of reflections, seemed to be a happy marriage. In a way they informed each other. My reflections kept me mindful of what I was thinking about. My therapy was given depth by the daily practice of that same mindfulness.

None of this was intentional, it just happened, and I never thought about it in this way at the time. Indeed, my understanding of Mindfulness as a specific therapeutic practice didn't occur until well after finishing this book. I knew from therapy that I had to be constantly alert about my thoughts, especially those unhelpful ones that might trigger either a manic or depressive episode, but that was it. I put this down to the mind and body being instinctively knowledgeable about what they need to survive.

Mindfulness is simply stopping and being present in the moment. It's not always easy to achieve, but when it does occur it makes life more vivid. Mindfulness also comes with a heightened sense of gratitude, in a way that always thinking of either the past or the future doesn't necessarily.

There are many good books on Mindfulness and many good counselors who can help you incorporate it into your life. This book, however, is not a 'How To', but an example of Mindfulness in action. Though created with no thought of a practical result, there was a deliberateness in the writing to leave mental room for the reader to have their own Mindful reflections. So it's the sort of book you can pick-up at any time, consider, then continue on your own path to recovery; with maybe a little extra hope on your side.

Some reflections talk directly to bi-polar, its symptoms and treatment. But the majority are simply thoughts that occurred to me as I gradually returned to health. The ruminations may be peculiar to me, but the subjects are able to be shared. In this way it hopefully has the benefit of group therapy, where you often learn more about yourself by listening to those around you.

Finally, I hope it occasionally makes you laugh. Therapy is often such a dry business, reaching deep into some of the most troubling aspects of our lives. I find being able to laugh at myself has made it easier.

While reading a book

While reading a book a page is turned and there is a stain from an old bookmark, left there for who knows how long. The bookmark itself is a thin slither of exercise book paper the width of two faint blue lines. The paper is browned, just like the stain it has left at an angle on the page. The bookmark wasn't seen before as it didn't protrude from the pages. Is it a book you tried to read but only got this far? Is it someone else's mark? Whichever way, it must have been some time ago to leave a stain like that. Has the book been waiting on the shelf for so long?

The sound of traffic in the morning

The sound of traffic in the morning tells me what time to get up. Through the night the cars are widely spaced. Before the dawn the spaces get smaller. I wait for the first light and the occasional truck's rumble. The cars are almost constant now with people going to work. On the weekends I still get up at the same time with my body tuned that way.

Chinese watercolors are painted that way for a reason

Chinese watercolors are painted that way for a reason. When you go to Guilin you will understand. Those paintings of mist covered rocky peaks with lakes, water buffalo and fishermen propelling themselves with long poles, could only be painted with soft daubs absorbed on fine rice paper or silk. Because that's what it looks like for real. It's as if a thin veil has been placed over your eyes and everything has this watery gentleness. Even from the town centre of 300,000 inhabitants, you quickly look beyond the ordinary buildings to some not-so-distant limestone peak, telling you people are the foreign element in this ancient landscape.

Not that the people are without their own history. Nearby are caves that housed the locals when the Japanese invaded. Up to 3,000 people in one cave not much bigger than a football field, reaching down through the dripping stalagmites, with fettered puddles and pools stale from human use. Imagine them holding silent, hands clasped over their babies' mouths, knowing that the enemy would slaughter and rape without compunction. At night the men would slip out in parties to gather what food they could - roots and handfuls of wild rice, hardly enough to keep them all from starvation.

Not all the history is so drear. Guilin has brought its artistry into the city with the construction of seven magnificent bridges over three interconnected lakes. Each of the bridges is different. One made of marble and beautifully carved. Another made of glass. Beautiful tea-house pagodas crop up along the shores. Sitting on the highest floor you can look out and see swans drifting, and people cycling and ambling along paths through flowering gardens. The menu of teas is almost confusing, and a treat when you open the lid of your pot to find a full chrysanthemum flower floating, as if upon its own pond.

In the local theatre there is a nightly performance very popular with tourists, who come mostly from around China and occasionally elsewhere. Guilin is a tourist city even for its own people. The show is a magnificent display of singing, music, acrobatics, dancing and drama, featuring performances and styles from all the different neighboring peoples. The audience flocks in from their giant tourist buses parked one on top of the other, making you wonder how they will find which bus is theirs when it's all over.

But for the truest taste of Guilin you must go to the art gallery, which doubles as a college for those aspiring to join the ranks of China's finest artists. Here the academy's master will silently demonstrate how the paper and ink are prepared, before gently flicking his wrist effortlessly, producing a picture of bamboo stalks with their leaves bending to the breeze. This image of gentle yielding is mirrored in the man who humbly bows before leaving.

If you should take the trip along the River Li to Yangshuo you will become absorbed in this seemingly painted landscape. Seven boats drift for five hours downstream in single file. You see fishermen using cormorants tied at the neck to make their catch. The birds duck into the water and capture the fish in their enormous beaks, but are unable to swallow because of their noose, forcing them to surrender their prey. Why is it you feel sad for the bird and not the fish?

Outside of Yangshuo you can witness a spectacle astounding in its proportions. By a lake, with whole peaks lit up as far as a kilometer away, a show begins with 200 fishermen bearing lanterns, who drift out of the darkness silently on their thin boats. A story is told of the lives of the people who are from around here. Red cloth is stretched out from one side of the lake to the other, forming fifty rows of waving sea. An ornate white wedding barge comes into sight, telling an ancient story of love and renewal.

The water that nourishes everything here is the stage. And always the peaks glow in the background, as hundreds of the locals end their day in the fields and on the waterways, by putting on a performance for more of those busloads of tourists.

When you leave, the fumes from so many buses make you cough. Your eyes sting and are awash with other tears.

It's hard to know

It's hard to know when my longest day began and ended, but it did take several days. It began in Thailand on a Saturday. I took the boat to catch the taxi that took me to the plane that flew me up from Krabi to Bangkok to catch the other plane that would fly all day to deliver me to Bahrain. It hadn't been much of a holiday in Krabi. I had gotten an ear infection in the first few days, and despite the idyllic setting I soon became bored, being on my own and surrounded by taunting water.

When I got home on the Saturday night there was a message for me that the next night I would be flying to London for a presentation. I went to bed tired from my long day's journey.

At work the next day (for religious purposes the week goes from Sunday to Thursday in the Middle East) there was plenty of catching-up to do and not enough time. When you run a big team and have been away for a week there's not a person who doesn't want a piece of you.

Taking the brief for the presentation was quick. We had been writing TV scripts for a particular brand for months and now was the time to front-up. The scripts we had been developing were meant for the Middle East, but at the last moment we had been invited to present to the global team, with the possibility that the scripts might go worldwide. All the different regions would be there presenting scripts. The rules of the presentation were that no storyboards were to be used, just the scripts as they were on paper. I had four scripts, so all I had to do was pack a bag and four sheets of paper. Telling me all this only took five minutes, so I could move on to another blindingly busy day, putting out the immediate fires and just running a quick hose over those that could smolder for a couple of days until my return. When the normal work day was done I went home, packed, and headed straight for the airport.

The flight was about seven hours so I got some sleep and ran over the scripts again to remind myself. When I got to Heathrow there was no car waiting for me from the hotel. I called them and they told me to catch a cab, which would have been fine, except there had just been a bomb scare and people were running towards the queue. While I patiently waited my turn I got my first message from my regional head of the brand, who was from Istanbul and whom I'd never met or even communicated with.

Eventually I got in a cab and continued to receive messages asking where I was at five minute intervals all the way to the hotel. As I was checking-in I received my final message, telling me I was on in twenty minutes. I got directions to our office from the hotel and asked them to send Eggs Benedict up with my bags. In the room I quickly hit the shower, wolfed down the eggs, got dressed, and grabbed my four bits of paper.

When I got to the boardroom of our London office, a quick 2-minute sprint away, there were about forty people. The room was all done-up with reminders of the brand – lots of product, blobs of plasticine in the brand's colour, previous work. A quick head count and calculation of flights and hotel bills told me this was about a quarter of million dollar meeting.

I was called over by my finally relieved Istanbul client. The presentation by the South American team was still going, and my heart sank a little. Not only did they have storyboards, they also had web ideas, and billboards, and print executions and an idea for a cartoon series. They finished to thunderous applause. It was my turn. I walked to the head of the long table, looked up at the room full of anonymous faces, placed my four pieces of paper on the table in front of me, and stepped back.

I never rehearse a presentation; my technique is simply to have a good opening line, knowing that since I did the work and understand it best, the rest will naturally follow. But this time, with all the rush, I had nothing, and don't know how the following came out. "In the Middle East we have just finished Ramadan."

I talked about what this meant in practical terms, and then went on to the implications, segueing these into our research findings and how these influenced the development of the scripts. Then I described the scripts, leaving the pages on the table. The audience was attentive throughout and applauded warmly at the end.

The rest of the day we sat through the presentations from the US, Asia Pacific, Europe and Africa. They produced prototypes of dolls, storyboard after storyboard, an idea for a pop group, social networking concepts. One team had produced an eight page newspaper, as if their campaign had already launched and what the press were saying about it. But I had done my job. At every break someone else would come up to me and want to talk about what life was like in the Middle East. I had lived there three months and had somehow managed to put myself up as an expert.

That night there was a dinner at the hotel and I wasn't going to let a little exhaustion hold me back. I was one of the first there and had the hotel set-up a small bar for me, where I mixed the cocktails I remembered from my old nightclub days as people came in. I managed to stay respectably long at the dinner, not being the first to leave or the last. That night I fell into the bed. But unfortunately my body clock was so out of sync with jetlag that I woke far too early.

Not to let a chance go by, I headed by tube into Covent Garden, to a shop I knew from when I had lived in London years before. The agency needed books desperately, so the team could broaden their thinking beyond the fare they were served-up each day in the Middle East. There was plenty of time to do this, as the day before us presenters had been told to keep out of the meeting until after lunch. At which point we would be told which scripts they had decided would be going into research. So by the time I'd gotten my books, had a wander around fondly familiar streets, and made my way back, it was judgment time.

Three scripts from New York, two from South America and one from the Middle East had been selected. They took us aside and briefed us on a conference call we would shortly be making to the worldwide head of the brand, when we would present the so-called winners. My Istanbul client was ecstatic. No script from the Middle East had ever been considered by the brand for worldwide release. The call to the worldwide head went smoothly enough, but it was awkward sitting in a chair with everyone behind you, while you talked into a camera with the boss' head on a screen just out of your eyeline.

With the meeting closed everyone headed back to the hotel for drinks. I had already checked-out in the morning and only had time for a couple before making my way back to the airport, where I again caught an overnight flight, going straight from the airport to the office to be in time for the start of the day.

It was Wednesday morning; I worked hard through the day and survived until Thursday night and the weekend. My colleagues treated it like I had been on one long holiday, and made me pay for my glutinous absence.

The commercial did get made. But with having to navigate fresh rounds of research, and my frequent late night fights with New York, plus all the extra months that process took, by the time it was finished no one even thought to celebrate. It had been a long day, and all for thirty seconds of TV.

You always have a boss

You always have a boss, no matter how high you go. You start by hating your boss and blaming them for everything. Then they make you a boss and you find that there are three bosses you now answer to, and all the decisions you hated when you weren't a boss you now realize you shouldn't have blamed your boss for. The higher you go, the more bosses you get. When you're a big boss you answer to the board. When you're the boss of bosses you answer to the shareholders. Shareholders think, "Have I put my money in the right place? Am I providing properly for my family? What's going to happen next?" They are their own boss, but they are still answering to somebody, even if it is themselves. And that can be harder.

'100 children' is my favourite Chinese motif

'100 children' is my favourite Chinese motif. It represents prosperity in the future. But this is not so important; it's the playfulness of the way each of the hundred children is portrayed. We have it as big embroidery, on a ceramic tile, on small embroidery, and on a glass globe painted from the inside. It's incredible to watch these globes painted through a hole in the bottom, with the finest of brushes, by very patient artists. We also have a larger globe of the Great Wall. They are all part of what we laughingly call Our Treasures.

We have three main hugs

We have three main hugs – two cuddling each other's backs, the third where her head rests on my chest. The last one feels more equal as we're both cuddling each other. I know she has had a bad night when I get up and go to the living room and find there is only one cigarette left in the packet; knowing I would be cranky if there were none.

Kookaburra's laughter

Kookaburra's laughter at the beginning of the day, or at the end, makes me smile. It tells me I am at home here in Australia. Some people think their laughter is mocking, but I think they're just glad to be around and happy to welcome and farewell each day for whatever it might bring. They're a funny looking bird, plump, with a beak that could crack a nut. So they seem somehow almost like a small animal and not a bird at all. And even when they're young they look sort of old, with their grey feathers and librarian's eyebrows. Old and wise, laughing and knowing.

When boxers have to put on a show

When boxers have to put on a show you know it's for publicity - wrestling amongst the microphones at a press conference. But how much is also trying to raise a rage, real or imagined, so they can hit someone they really don't know?

Is there anything more hateful?

Is there anything more hateful than homework? It was the best thing to leave behind when school was done. Freedom is going to work without a briefcase full of Maths problems.

Test cricket

Test cricket is named 'Test' cricket because that's what it is - the test of the player. What other sport forces you into the spotlight for five days? Each night the game hangs over the players' heads. While sitting at dinner, or alone in hotel rooms, it's still there. It can only wear on you.

The final batting team always finds it hard to maker big runs in their second innings. The pitch is worn, the ball plays tricks, they have often been out in the field longer than the bowling team, also the end and its promise of rest is in sight, no matter what the result.

Or perhaps the real difficulty of the last day's play is something they saw laying on their solitary bed watching last night's movie - when the villain, and not the hero, got away.

When furniture arrives in flat boxes

When furniture arrives in flat boxes and you have to make it yourself, you always get it wrong the first time, even after reading the instructions. This never bothers me as it always happens this way. I smile and start undoing what has only just been done. What's to get so frustrated about? If only life were this simple.

The worst sore

The worst sore is one made by acid. You get a scab like a crater with a dark pool at the bottom, rimmed by swollen red flesh that sometimes itches. It takes months to heal and scars for much much longer. It would have only taken me a few seconds to put on the gloves, which is no time at all in geological terms.

My sneezes

My sneezes are so loud that you can hear them echo off the concrete walls in our living room. I can't stop them and they go right through my body, starting deep inside and rushing out to create a mist that lingers in the air longer than the spray of a sprinkler. Sometimes you can smell them.

If I never see another cathedral

If I never see another cathedral or temple or mosque or Buddha statue I'll be fine. Worshippers are usually asking for something, which you can tell by the intensity of their supplications. In my experience thanks is usually given lightly. Plus I'm no fan of religion.

The buildings do a good job of perpetrating the myth. Different light, non-human spaces, different sounds, different smells. The setting is otherworldly, encouraging otherworldly thoughts, and dwarfing what you are.

I was once in a gothic cathedral in Paris and it was so dark, lighted only by distant candles, the ceiling so far away, the air so silent and incense heavy, it was not of this earth. It was awesome and probably the last time I was impressed by these places.

That was my first time in Paris, when I was young and discovered it was the poor man's city. You only needed to walk out onto the streets for a day of endless entertainment. Thank heavens.

How strange the mind is

How strange the mind is, the way you can read the pages of a book while thinking about something else entirely, then suddenly realize you haven't taken in anything at all, even though your eyes have not missed a single word. That's when you have to go back and start again, concentrating this time on something your brain has already covered and stored in some way, and yet every word seems fresh.

Anthony Peck

Guilty Pleasures

Eating cereal at any time other than breakfast.
Watching sport late into the night even though you know it will
make you useless at work the next day.
Smoking when you shouldn't.
Not being found out for a lie.
Peeing outdoors.
Changing in or out of your swimmers in the car park, even
though you might get caught naked.
Having the last bit of any sweet.
Buying another book when you know you promised to stop.
Reading a really bad book on a beach holiday.
Taking three showers in a day.
Watching a movie at breakfast.
Wearing pyjamas all day.

The best thing that ever happened to me

The best thing that ever happened to me was being diagnosed with manic depression. They call it bi-polar now, but I prefer manic depression, because they're emotive words and capture the power of the thing. They probably changed the name to make it less scary, but it can be scary. They may have changed it because it is semantically more accurate – you go from pole to pole – whereas manic depression sounds like you have a depression that is out of control, when in fact you are sometimes manic and sometimes depressed. Another reason could be that by sounding less dramatic it recognizes that you're not always one or the other. There are periods when you are completely in the middle and other times when you are a little more of one or a little more of the other. Making it sound less dramatic also helps other people not be afraid of you or it. This is important. There is nothing to be afraid of if you manage it properly. And you don't want anyone to be afraid of you, or for you to be afraid of yourself. Manic depression is a big tag to carry, whereas bi-polar just sounds like a condition you have, like asthma. It's funny that I can see the positive side of calling it bi-polar so clearly, yet still prefers manic depression. Truth be told, I often flick from one to the other when describing it. To everyone else I call it bi-polar. To myself it's sometimes bi-polar and sometimes manic depression. It sounds like a very bi-polar way to think. But I will stick with manic depressive here because of the circumstances in which I was diagnosed. Or not.

It started with a tingling down my right arm and a pain in my shoulder. I knew what this was, it was my neck. Years ago I had had a small part of my spine cut out to free trapped nerves. It had been horrible, leaving a big scar down the back of my neck. These were the same symptoms and I didn't want to go through it again. I got the tests and the results weren't good, so I flew back to Australia to have another operation. This time they went through my throat, removed two discs, then built a cage around the area and screwed in a piece of titanium. The first neck operation had taken six weeks to recover from, but this time I was determined to get back to work quicker.

I was living and working in Bahrain and a presentation for a new piece of business was coming up two weeks after the operation that I was determined to make. The agency depended on me and my boss was sending me text messages that they were waiting for me. Nine days after the operation I got on a plane and flew back from Australia with a foam collar around my neck. The day after arriving I went into the office and put on a good show. I walked around for about an hour chatting with people, but when I got home collapsed and slept like a baby. The next day I called and said I wouldn't be able to make the following day's presentation.

But still I wanted to get back. I was lucky as a colleague and friend lived just down the road and looked after me when he wasn't at work. But he was moving back to Jordan to run another agency, and at the end of the week left.

Over the next four weeks I received just four visits from my colleagues. I couldn't drive and had to live on home delivery. The days were filled with sleep and television and I became depressed. I started to hear voices calling my name, but there was no one there.

One day I found my neck was getting infected. It was until the evening that I called around to my colleagues to get one of them to take me to the hospital. It took several calls before one of them answered. He came and took me to the hospital, where my neck was examined and they said they would keep me for a few days on an antibiotic drip. And then they said they thought there might be something else wrong as well. I was shaking uncontrollably, twitching and started to cry. They called in the psychiatrist who said I was depressed. He said they would keep me and look after me and give me anti-depressants. He was a nice man from Iraq. I felt relieved when they took me up to the ward. The colleague who brought me to the hospital was very concerned and caring and said he would tell them at work.

The next day my boss came and said to just get better. I said I would go back to Australia when I was well enough and recover from the depression there. I thought that would speed things up. Then I got a call from our Regional boss who in a friendly way told me to stop being depressed. He even put his wife on the phone. They were all being very nice to me.

Soon after getting out of the hospital I flew. I couldn't get out quick enough. The month alone had been a type of lonesome hell. The anti-depressants were starting to take effect and I was feeling buoyant. I spent my first week in Australia at my brother's house, but he and his wife were away, so my three lovely nephews and their girlfriends looked after me. Then one of my dearest and oldest friends came and got me for a few days of sunshine and wave watching in her house near the beach. After that I went to a health retreat on her recommendation, where each day I was feeling better and better. So good in fact, that when I left after just a week, I decided to fly home that very night. I went to my brother's house to say goodbye, and my ever-loving aunt and uncle even dropped by to wish me well before my brother drove me to the airport.

On the way home I stopped over in Hong Kong, and even made a trip into China to my favourite spa. This turned into a major shopping spree, which resulted in my having to pay the equivalent of another passenger ticket for my excess baggage. Shopping is something we bi-polars love. That and buying lots of gifts. They call it 'Grandiosity', but in the family we laughingly call it 'Gigantism'.

What a high I rode as I returned to the office. I had everything planned, I would take over the world, we would be the greatest advertising agency ever, and we would look after and train our people like never before. For two weeks I worked day and night at a speed that was frightening everyone around me. My boss had been too true to his word and they had all waited for me. And by that I mean they had almost stopped working until I could be there to make all the decisions. So there was a lot of catching-up to do. On top of that I moved house. And when I wasn't busily working, I managed to move everything in and have it all set-ups within forty-eight hours. I barely slept.

Then one day my boss came in and said that for our next new business pitch our Regional Creative Head would be coming to join us again. I had already been through this once and didn't want to repeat it. Having someone regional there was always heavy going. A pitch is difficult enough on its own, add someone who everyone is afraid of or intimidated by, and it only gets worse.

Indiscretion is another thing common to people with bi-polar, and didn't I let my boss have it one evening? I not only covered the problems with having the regional head there, but also the way I was so poorly looked after in a country where I was alone and barely visited by the only people I knew when I had been so ill. I threw in a demand for a pay rise. I threw everything I had at him. He walked away understandably stung, and silent.

The next day the Regional boss came into the office. My own boss told me that later on that day this head honcho wanted to talk with me about why I didn't want the Regional Creative Head there for the upcoming pitch. I knew this was death. It was the Regional boss' policy that we should all act like one big family, though this was a very flexible policy depending on who he considered to be in or out of the 'family'. My boss had obviously told him of my objection. I asked him if we would also address the other issues I had raised so vehemently the evening before. He said we would do that another time.

Remember I was flying. I decided I couldn't control myself in front of the big boss. It was an argument I was only going to lose. So I told one of my colleagues that I was going home and would come back when the agency had sorted its shit out. My phone rang at the appointed time for the afternoon's meeting, but I chose not to answer, for the very reasons I wasn't going to attend a meeting that would only see me buried. No message was left.

The following morning I went straight to my psychiatrist. I told him how I had been behaving. I called my boss from the psychiatrist's office, when my boss told me that by leaving the office I had effectively resigned and that all the staff had been told of this the evening before. I said how I was calling from my psychiatrist's office and that I realized I had been behaving strangely and was doing something about it. He said it was all over, there was nothing more to discuss.

When I put down the phone a switch got flicked inside me. I was now watching myself from the outside. The psychiatrist gave me a prescription for muscle relaxants. I took this to the hospital pharmacy and got it filled. I got in the car and drove home numb. I knew I was going to kill myself. When I got home I swallowed all the muscle relaxants, plus all the valium I could lay my hands on and anything else that might speed me on my way. I got into a hot bath. I may not have been myself, but I was sure I had taken enough pills to do the job.

The next thing I know I am in a hospital bed. It wasn't the pills. I had jumped off the top of my building, four floors up. I broke everything – both feet, left ankle, right pelvis, five ribs, punctured lung, middle of my back, both collar bones, right shoulder, neck. I had collected a bougainvillea tree on the way down, which left a lot of scratches with its long thorns, but probably saved me from death. I had been in hospital for four days before I have my first memory, which was one of my closest colleagues, the wonderful Sam, telling me that my family was coming to get me. I had and have no memory of the great leap. My brother, my aunt, and my now wife couldn't get there quick enough for my liking. When they finally did arrive I was relieved beyond all imagining. In the meantime, Sam was often by my side and doing everything she could for me.

To describe my time in this first hospital during my recovery is not easy. I was in and out of consciousness, having wild hallucinations, struggling with difficult conditions. My memory is scattered and incomplete, and I have had to rely on others' accounts to make any sense of most of it. But I will try to cover what it was like.

To begin, I was found by the security guard from one of the buildings opposite where I lived. He had been walking past my fence when he heard what he thought was a chicken. He looked over and saw me lying naked on the ground, curled-up and whimpering. He quickly got my housekeeper, who called for an ambulance and covered me with a blanket for modesty. She also called the colleague who had taken me to the hospital with the infected neck and who had tried to call on me that day but, receiving no reply after knocking on my door, had waited in his car outside for some time before finally going home. Though not before leaving his number with my housekeeper, who lived in her own separate quarters attached to the side of the house. My colleague had been worried about my behavior and was more than a little alarmed at my supposed resignation.

Apparently I was quite coherent in those first four days, even though I have zero memory of them. A few colleagues came to visit, and I jokingly told them how they could all improve. I was still on the job. I had also remembered that a friend from Hong Kong would be visiting, and sent them off to the airport to pick her up. She stayed for the appointed weekend, which was meant to be fun, but was instead spent by my bedside in Intensive Care.

The hospital had me in restraints, as I apparently kept trying to get out of bed. One of my first memories, when I was now in a ward, was seeing my arms black and blue with bruising from the struggling I had put up with the wrist bands. I had actually broken free of them during one of my hallucinations, where I had imagined being taken to an apartment against my will by an evil woman, who I later recognized as one of my nurses, and where I was afraid of being experimented on. The trip to the apartment was probably the ambulance ride. In that hallucination I remember calling for scissors to cut a cake, knowing that I was really going to use them to cut myself free. But I have a vivid recollection of seeing a cake on a counter and of kicking at the evil woman, which I probably did for real to the nurse who, once

I became somewhat cognizant, was always unsurprisingly very curt with me.

The first face of my trio of rescuers that I remember seeing was Camille's. She took my hand and I looked up and there she was like an angel. Then my brother and aunt appeared at the bottom of the bed, before moving up to kiss me. Before then I had never known how important other people are. Having now been totally stripped of the independence I had lived and sworn by, I was happier than ever. Because for the first time I knew that everything would be alright, not thanks to me and my efforts, but because other people loved me. My Aunt Jan gave me a rich mauve blanket from my cousin Natalie, which I wasn't to let go of for some time. She also had some photos of the family, that she stuck in places I could see them.

I was still racing, and over the following days continued to talk rapidly, almost brilliantly. I was devising advertising campaigns and asking my visitors to write them down. In the meantime their lot was far from a happy one. Besides being concerned for me they were struggling to get me out of that hospital and into a better one. There was even an effort amongst the hospital staff to have me put into a psych ward which my fearless team had to fight off, knowing that if I ever went in there I was never coming out.

The hospital wasn't the best facility. Built for six hundred it housed over a thousand. Twenty-three of us shared the one urine bottle, which the nurses only gave a cold rinse before handing it to the next person. I got an infection off that. Getting a bed-pan was also a problem. The nurses would never come, and when they did it would be too late. Sometimes I would spend hours laying in my own shit. One of the psychiatrists, a nice young girl who was a friend of a friend, came and asked me about this shitting myself, as it was one of the reasons they were giving for sending me to the psych ward. But I told her it was just that no one would bring me a pan in time. This gave her the ammunition she needed to keep me safe from a worse fate.

What I remember feeling about life in the ward was just that I wanted to get out. I told my family that as soon as they arrived. I wanted out that very day. For some reason I blamed my aunt for me not getting out immediately. "You should be happy, you got just what you wanted," I told her. I love her so much I wonder how I could have been like that to her. But I was quite mad.

The problem, it turned out, was that no other hospital in The Kingdom of Bahrain had the equipment to deal with the problems that might arise with me physically. The punctured lung was a problem, and they really didn't know what else might be wrong. They had identified tearing to my liver and kidneys, and who knows what else was going on? Their uncertainty was no doubt heightened by the paucity of their knowledge and their own poor working conditions. X-rays were taken at bedside, with just a quick warning to anyone who didn't have to be there to get out and avoid the radiation. It was that slipshod.

Every day my family fought to get me out, running from office to office, stealing x-rays, and bringing in the psychiatrist I had been seeing from the other hospital. Meanwhile I was quite insane. There were hallucinations of being in a Thai prisoner-of-war camp, of being in a French bath house, of being made to wait naked and strapped to the wall for hours and hours while beautiful women luxuriated in front of me in a steam room. There were animations on the ceiling that I pointed out to anyone who cared to listen; marvelous images of water drops turning into flowers. I believed that at night they spun the room over so that the ceiling became the wall opposite, and they would pump in experimental gases. One night I believed that the nurses had invited all their friends in and they were standing around shooting-up drugs and having a wild old time.

There were a lot of noises at night anyway. The guy next to me was on life support and I asked for the constantly sucking machine to be turned off. Bottles were constantly being smashed into a recycle bin right underneath a nearby window. Visitors would come at all hours and talk in loud groups. I told a nurse to tell one group that if they didn't shut up I would take them on one at a time or singly, it was up to them.

I was no great fun either, and my fellow patients apparently wanted me out as much as I wanted out. I would pull off my oxygen mask, tore a tube out that went down to my draining lung, ripped out stitches in the back of my head and neck. Grappled the bandages off my feet and picked the stitches apart. Nurses would come to my bed and there would be blood on my fingers, hands and sheets again. I would phone Camille in the middle of the night during the hallucinations, and she would come and calm me down.

But for all that, my fellow convalescents became friendly with me, as did some of their regular guests. I recall one group standing around my bed - construction workers from Bangladesh or India or Pakistan - they were all smiling and telling me they were praying for me. They seemed very sorry for me, these very same men who I would pity daily as I drove to and from work. I would watch them sweltering in the forty-two degree heat, knowing they were no more than indentured slaves, who would take two years to pay-off their debt for flying over, and for their room and board in appalling conditions. Many of these men would commit suicide, having no hope on this earth. These are the things you don't read about the booming Gulf.

I made one friend in that hospital, the man who came and washed me. At that stage they had no idea of how much of me was broken and he was very rough, flipping me from one side to the next. I would scream and he would laugh and try to get me to remember a sentence in Arabic, which I finally did conquer and can even now remember, "Shukram yakiman mishtookra". Those who speak Arabic will know that it's wrong, but that's my phonetic attempt. Apparently it means something like, "Thankyou, one day I will be as good a hospital cleaner as you."

Between my aunt and the psychiatrist I was diagnosed with manic depression. My aunt has a Masters in Psychology, and I believe it was really her and not the psychiatrist who could see what was going on. They took me off the anti-depressants that were heightening the problem. And with much maneuvering and slight of hand, I was eventually transferred to a better hospital after seventeen days, the one where they had treated my infected neck and my 'depression'. I can't remember the ambulance ride, but apparently I begged them to use the siren, which they did.

Besides my family's constant fight to have me moved, there was also the delicate situation of my having broken Islamic law. Suicides are in a lot of trouble. Camille was interrogated at police headquarters in a scene that sounds like something out of a movie. Fortunately she got through it ok, and when it was all over one of the interrogating police took her to one side and offered all his help, assuring her that I would be allowed out of the country safely. All she had to do was give him an exact departure date and call him the day before to confirm we were leaving. So now there is apparently one country I am banned from ever entering again.

It seems I came almost completely to my senses once I was in the familiar surrounds of the other hospital. Originally designed as a five star hotel, this was bliss. My own room, a view of the harbour, tv, a comfortable bed I could control myself, and lots of familiar faces amongst the nurses. And food. In the other hospital I hadn't eaten anything until my family arrived. A tray of jelly, something mashed, and a soda was left on a tray out of my reach daily, so a pile of these were stacked there when my family arrived. I think we counted over a dozen cans of Coke.

I stayed in the new hospital for six days. My aunt went home almost as soon as I was safely ensconced. Leaving Camille and my brother Matthew to flick through the channels with me, watching the limited fare available on Middle Eastern TV. I was able to get out of bed and have showers with Camille's assistance, and later on my own. There was also the first of a series of phone calls from a friend in Hong Kong, for which I will always be grateful.

I remember all that time. It's like a switch had been thrown the moment I arrived in the new hospital. I was now on antipsychotic drugs and anti-bi-polar drugs. Everything was becoming clearer.

When I was finally well enough they took me home, where I spent my time between my bed and the TV. Matthew stayed for about a week of that, and we even managed to get out to a restaurant, the gold souk, and another souk at Isa Town where we bought rugs. We didn't know my feet or ankle were broken then, so it was painful for me to walk, but there was an insistence that I get up and about to help me recover.

I say this was the best thing to happen to me even though it may not sound that way. But it was. For the first time in my life my thoughts were coming steadily, in an orderly fashion, not racing around and butting-in and chasing down blind alleys. One day Camille was sitting on my bed with me, holding my hand, and I suggested we marry. It was the most obvious thing in the world. We had been together on and off for years, and now that my head was clear it seemed odd that we hadn't married. We had spent most of our lives together with me being mad, why wouldn't we be together till the end while I was now sane? She quietly agreed.

What followed was the packing-up of the house, final farewells, and all the detail of moving country. Then we were on a plane and home. We got married four months later in a beautiful ceremony at Camille's mother's house by Sydney Harbour.

I have the best medical treatment and continue to rejoice in my new brain. Being manic depressive had ruled my life and made things very difficult for me from a very early age. It didn't take long to look back and be able to map all the ups and downs and their affects. It's a classic case shared by many, though it is important to understand that everyone's version of the disorder is different, which I learnt from meeting other manic depressives. My final episode was extreme, but it was what I finally needed to set things right. There is a wonderful ease about being able to think straight that comes with the drugs. And now I can manage my thoughts to prevent a repeat - allowing them to come and go as they please, flowing like a river, skirting rocky obstacles instead of trying to take them on, knowing that one day even these I will wear down. It was the best thing to ever happen to me, whichever way you look at it.

The only problem

The only problem with incense is the ash it leaves. You get these really cute little holders with just a neat little hole to hold the stick, but where does the ash go? Everywhere. The Chinese have great incense burners for spirals of incense that capture the ash in their container. But not us. We produce little one centimeter cubes made out of marble or some other rock, with absolutely no care for the ash.

Or there are the long wooden ones turned-up at the end, where the incense hangs horizontally and is meant to fall into a neat groove made in the wood. But the stick rarely hangs cleanly over the groove, or even the wood for that matter. And even the slightest breeze leaves you with incense everywhere.

We have one of the Chinese burners, but the spirals can be difficult to manage, because they're stuck together and often break off mid-way through burning, because the spirals are too close together and the ember catches the next spiral along.

We haven't solved the problem of the incense yet, but we're working on it.

We rarely use the main lights

We rarely use the main lights, preferring lamps instead. My favourite is the one by the black bean plant that creates leaf shadows on the wall. When a breeze blows it brings movement into the room, the leaves gently bend, curtains sway. Amongst so many solid things the fluidity is refreshing. The main lights are used only when we seem to have lost something.

When body surfing

When body surfing, dolphin-entries are the most fun. Wearing flippers, you duck down as the wave approaches, then kick hard just as it passes over you, shooting out of the face of the wave with its full force behind you. This way you not only avoid being dumped, you also get to fly like Superman, if only for a second. Plus there's almost no limit to the size of waves you can catch.

The Jesus-entry is when you spread your arms crucifixion-style at the crest of the wave, then spin down the face, leaving an artistic looping wash behind you.

Backward-entries are possible on smaller waves, and have the added thrill of not knowing when the force of the wave will hit you, or where you're going.

Chest out, head held high, gives you a great bounce when you come down on a dumper.

One day a woman came up to me on the shore as I was getting out from a particularly fun session, and said she wished I could teach her husband. I can't remember how I learned, except for the dolphin-entry. That came from my friend The Shark. They call him that because of the way he plays pool.

Watching TV

Watching TV the sound goes up when the ads come on. Do they think we're more likely to buy if they yell at us? My father was always yelling at us. It ended-up no one liked him.

Whenever I can

Whenever I can I eat with one hand. It saves on washing-up and somehow makes the food taste better and more real, without the metallic taste. It's common in many cultures. Salads can always be eaten with your hands; fish is good, anything eaten with bread, all fruit. Steaks are less attractive, but if you cut them up first it's ok. But then you've got a knife and fork you have to wash as well as your hand, so what's the point?

When my stomach's empty

When my stomach's empty it sets up its own orchestra. Not just in the stomach, but all through my digestive system. It's not a proper orchestra, because it produces no real music. There's no syncopation, no melody. It's just like they're warming-up. And it doesn't always make a sound. Sometimes I just feel a foot testing the peddles on a piano down there somewhere. Then there's a little trombone to the bottom left, a quick drum roll near my kidneys, someone clearing their throat where my gall bladder used to be. The warm-up intensifies until it seems they're just about to go into action, and then "Boom!" it's over, my stomach muscles cramp. Like an old conductor collapsing on stage, just as he was about to raise the baton.

The first meal after being hungry is not as good as you'd think. There's been too much anticipation. And you tend to gulp it down, so it barely brushes your taste buds. Then your stomach cries out - having been shrunken first and now force-fed to busting. Slow meals are delicious. But you need an equally slowed mind. Never eat standing. Never eat for fuel.

Eat for eating, sweep the floor for the satisfaction of sweeping the floor, and when you lay down for a siesta, let you're last thought be of the comfort of your sheets and the softness of your pillow.

She doesn't know

She doesn't know most of the time that's she's singing. Not full-on songs, but little snippets, or melodies made-up to go with what she's doing. Sometimes she's the strings, sometimes the dum-de-dum drums. There's a lot of singing when she's in the kitchen. Some when she's working on her computer. The bathroom gets a good go. Anywhere really. It doesn't matter she doesn't know, I never stop her. I think it means she's happy.

The company of a dog

The company of a dog is something I have grown to appreciate later in life. My father was afraid of dogs and I grew up with the same fear. It was only getting to know dogs through my aunt and uncles' pets that I have come to love them.

Clyde was a British Bulldog who had led a hard life, spending most of his limited years in a car yard on a main road and never touching grass. The first time he trod on it he was terrified. Whenever anyone outside the family visited he would make a point of shitting in front of the guest room. But how could you get angry with such a dog? He needed ear drops, eye drops, and was such a regular at the vet that my uncle described him as Platinum, like a frequent flyer.

Now they have a black Labradoodle named Max. There is no smarter dog. When I have been sick he has known and come and sat with me. Even in the middle of winter, when I have had to go outside for a cigarette, he has always come out with me.

My cousin Natalie also has a Labradoodle, but Ruby is very excitable and no match for Max, who keeps him at paws-length.

Cousin Shane always has a British Bulldog, currently it's David. Recently he got de-sexed and Shane says he has lost his spirit along with his balls.

Sometimes we get to mind a little white Bijon Freise who belongs to Camille's mother's neighbour. Scruffy is very shy, and also very gentle. If you're gentle with him he can be quite affectionate. The other night I had my hand resting on his back and he reached out with his paw and placed it on my leg.

Proof-reading has become a lost art

Proof-reading has become a lost art, which is a shame as it has its own pleasure and needn't be treated as a chore. Now people let the software do the job, producing its own faults. A word may be spelled correctly, but what if it's the wrong word? For instance, what if you accidentally type 'can' when you mean 'man'? They're both correct spellings of a word, so the spell-checker won't pick-up what is actually a very obvious mistake.

Proper proofing requires reading both forwards and back. Reading forwards you check the grammar and catch some of the spelling mistakes. When you read backwards there is no sense, so you are forced to read each word on its own, and pick-up the spelling mistakes you missed reading forwards, when your mind may have made corrections in the flow of reading that you didn't even know about.

Proper proofing also has its own language, with its lexicon of symbols signifying the various corrections. A proofed sheet can look quite artistic in its own way, so that you can be tempted to publish with the marks left on.

Anthony Peck

I am always happy

I am always happy to see my psychologist. I go in a little nervous about what I must face, but never walk away without a good result. Each time I go I am a little less nervous and a little more happy. It must be working.

Even though I love water

Even though I love water I much prefer to be in it than on it. Whether it is still water, such as a river or a lake, or the ocean, I find it cruel to be on a boat or a kayak. The water is right there, but I'm not in it. What's the point? The ocean is best of all. You can surf, body surf, dive, snorkel. You play with the water. Still water is too predictable, except when you swing on a rope and are not sure when to let go. But that's you and not the water.

The people of Papua New Guinea

The people of Papua New Guinea have a very particular smell, and though I have not lived there since I was a small child, I can detect it from a great distance. It is a delicious smell in my memory, bringing back a time when I was especially happy.

I spent my days with the men building the road nearby, when they would pile their wheelbarrows high with rocks then sit me on top and wheel me down the hill, returning with me in the otherwise empty barrow. I guess I was their mascot. One day one of the men cut himself badly and refused to go to the hospital without me.

Having white hair at that time I was separated out for special attention. We were there for two years and I wonder how much of it I actually spent on my own feet. The locals carried me everywhere. There are old slides of people surrounding me, some holding me aloft.

The first memory I have of being back in Australia was standing by my mother, who was talking to someone I couldn't see over our back fence. The fence was wood and completely alien to me, as was the fact that I was being left out of the conversation with no one there to hold me up so I could join in. In New Guinea I was included in all conversations, whether with the bishop, or the nuns where my brothers went to school, or anyone child or adult. And Tar-Moon our houseboy was always there to help me. If he had been at that fence he would surely have lifted me up. It's a bad memory for me, the first time I felt left out. Our family kept closely to itself and we went to school some distance away, never getting to know any of the other neighbourhood children, or even our own cousins. So I increasingly felt isolated and my hair lost its whiteness and turned to a sandy, almost dirty brown.

Now if I smell a New Guinean I always go up and start a conversation - any excuse to stay near that glorious smell.

A house without photos

A house without photos can feel lonely. Photos are not there for guests but for the inhabitants. Without them a person can seem heartless, or even suspicious, but this may be overstepping the mark.

A rainy day

A rainy day after a period of sunny days can make you regret putting off the things you should have done.

The first sunny day after a lot of rain can be one of the best days of all.

Days that are sometimes sunny and sometimes cloudy, sometimes warm and sometimes cold, can make you feel unbalanced.

Windy days are infuriating. The wind gets in your ears, tosses your hair across your face, tears at your clothes, batters you. That night your skin feels sore and dry, and still the wind screeches for attention against your windows.

A great storm is a cause for celebration, as it puts on such a fantastic show. Plus you have every excuse to just stay indoors and weather it.

Drizzling rain lets you walk without an umbrella and enjoy the gentle spray.

To ignore the weather and always go on as if nothing changes is like having a gift you never unwrap.

Old stopwatches

Old stopwatches are the best, forget your digital ones. An old stopwatch lets you watch the time as the hand sweeps. With a digital how can your eyes keep track of the whirling numbers? Time occupies a space on an old stopwatch, so you can almost feel the dimensions of it. If you're timing a speech of a fixed length you can see where you should slow down or speed up. The same goes with training for any sort of race. Digital gives you a beginning and an end, when it's what happens in-between that counts.

When someone fails to show-up

When someone fails to show-up at an agreed time it can be very upsetting, especially in a foreign country. It's not yourself you worry about, but what could have happened to the other person. When they do finally appear, your concern can come out as anger. Now what was planned as a pleasant excursion becomes a day of trying to bridge the gap of hurt. Thank heavens we now have mobile phones.

We've moved so much

We've moved so much that we have every different type of electrical plug. I've even stopped trying to change them over. So every time we go to plug-in something new we have to find an adaptor. This makes all the sockets look quite dangerous, but they're not really.

It's one of the things we're always warned about, like running with scissors and losing an eye. But how often do you see a person with one eye, let alone one who lost it on the end of scissors? Then there's not swimming for at least half an hour after you've eaten. That one's probably to give parents some peace, before they have to go back to the duty of watching that their children don't drown.

Trying to make the world too safe takes the fun out. Even though it drives me crazy looking for the right adaptor, it at least reminds me of where we've been, and all the unforgettable adventures.

If you watch the news

If you watch the news we're all being ripped-off, or we're all going to die, or the enemy is just around the corner. But that's not my experience. People are generally good. And those that leave you with a bad feeling are often people with their own problems, and for those we should have empathy rather than animosity.

There's hardly a person I've met who I didn't think was really ok. It makes you wonder why this world of imagined fear has been created? Yet everyday there is the good. There is the good in billions of car trips taken without people deliberately trying to kill each other. There we are with a large piece of sophisticated machinery and yet we somehow, in most instances, avoid hurting each other. Go to the supermarket and you will find good when a person with a large trolley of groceries at the checkout lets someone in front of them with just a handful of things. Good is ubiquitous, hurtfulness rare.

It is a habit of mine to talk with whoever is in my vicinity - at shops, bus queues, anywhere really. This could be either madness or presumption. And yet there has never been a single instance where my promptings for conversation have been rejected. This is part of the Good. We want to talk with each other, to connect. We are not afraid, because away from the TV screen and amongst real people we know we are safe. But we're fighting the demands of 24 hour news here, and they've got to fill the time somehow.

To help me go to sleep

To help me go to sleep I have two very special memories. One is of a beautiful wave I caught in Uluwatu, Bali. A beautiful barreling left-hander. I was inside the whole time, surrounded by the glassy green, in the sweet spot where sound gets blocked-out. I shot out high at the end of the tube, and then flicked down the face to skirt the white wash that had broken before me, and catch the last bit of unbroken face. I rode a few more waves after that, and on the way to the shore an old surfer on a long plank said as he paddled past me, "I saw that tube you rode." Maybe it was his compliment that made me remember it especially. But I ride that wave over and over until sleep washes over.

The other memory is of a tee-shot I made on a day of bad golf. It was a straight par three that my uncle and his cousin's husband had dropped short on using irons. I took a three wood and smacked it. It started left then faded in right as if I had meant it to, dropped just short of the green, and rolled on until it was ten feet from the hole.

It's not like I think of just one of these memories on any given night, I always think of them both. In psychology they call that Self-Nurturing.

There are fast recoveries and slow recoveries

There are fast recoveries and slow recoveries. Fast recoveries are an instant, a moment's epiphany when rushes of pain or terror or fear are quickly relieved, and you burst out of that dark tunnel into the light. They are glorious and can seem worth the trouble preceding them. They can even be addictive, encouraging you to do things you know you shouldn't, because somewhere in the back of your mind you know the pay-off is going to be there and worth it. It may be what makes us hold our breathe for as long as we can underwater, or let our fingers be torn to shreds on the climb up a mountain. It can even be provoking a lover's tiff, or the ripping-off of a band aid, or the plucking of an eyebrow, or tearing at a scab.

Slow recoveries are to be avoided at all costs. It isn't just that time loses all meaning, but that you begin to doubt yourself. Am I really sick? Could I be doing more? Pain will quickly stop you, but aren't you more than pain? No longer a person but a patient, your conversations soon dry-up. "I was a person once, really...", but you forget that person along with everyone else it seems.

And you know it isn't going to suddenly end. There will be no triumph. Milestones are all you've got; stumbling along a highway you used to drive at speed, only checking occasionally to see that you're not over the limit, not for the sake of your safety, but to avoid a ticket. Maybe that's why they call it the road to recovery. But the landscape rarely changes. Home or the doctor's.

There are no outbursts. The frustration is a slow burner. A sudden rage will do no good, and besides, it never reaches that point. There's always the next meal, or shower, or TV show. Better to set your mind to neutral, accept re-runs, watch that you don't eat too much and get fat in your immobility.

No book will be written of your recovery, no monument raised. You're in it, that's all. Of course there are some wounds that will never heal, but even these came from before the recovery, when your willfulness told you anything was possible.

I rarely remember a face

I rarely remember a face
And worse with names
The mirror looks back
Wonders how I've aged
Time has stolen
Shames mounted
In a blurr
I don't come out very well.

My mind has played tricks
I can't recall
Or hold back
What might have been
Is not up to me
Seems it never was
My place to stand tall
Was never mine.

How I gloried
Ran amok
Was loved
Took flight
Hollow victories
Might fallen
Lost my place
Thumbs black with searching
What was never there.

Or there are patches
Tatters
Sewn into spaces
A fist could pass through
Which would have once
Seemed sky bound
Electric
Wounds.

These gaps
Now grieved
Like air
Once breathed
To never pass breathe again
Or waves
Magnificent
Forgotten
Terrible bubbles
On my shore.

The printer dances

The printer dances its own little dance before going to work, as if revving-up before taking on the challenge of dedicating thoughts to paper. It's a sort of jig that goes unseen, but is given away by machinery taps and slides heard from inside the casing. "You go over there." "No, you go over there, I'm staying right here." The bits have thespian squabbles before settling down. "This guy's crazy," they think. "Why couldn't we be attached to a calculator instead?"

One of my favourite pictures

One of my favourite pictures is in our bedroom. It's a classic Chinese watercolour of bamboo bending in the wind. You will see such paintings everywhere in China, the motif familiar from ancient Taoist teachings. The bamboo is strong, but flexible enough to weather even the wildest wind, it never breaks. Strong yet pliant– it could be a motto for Chinese pragmatism. One quiet step backwards may be more useful than attempting a charge doomed to failure.

But this particular painting is a very special one. When we show it to people they remark on how beautifully it has been done, the leaves stretching out along a broad horizontal unpainted paper background.

I bought it off the artist right on the street in Zhu Hai, just over the land border from Macau. She was sitting on a piece of plastic on a footpath cracked and crowded, her brushes in an old coffee jar, her paper stretched out before her. That someone with that much talent should have to work under such conditions is amazingly wrong. If she lived somewhere more prosperous she would have a studio and show in galleries. The sweeps of her brush, each artful caress, producing its own perfect leaf. More extraordinary still, she has no arms. It's all done using her feet.

When I got around to having it framed I was warned that the paper would wrinkle. I had it done anyway, and guess what? The wrinkles of the paper are as if the wind is not only in the painting, but also runs through the painting, ever-rippling on the wall. It couldn't be more perfect.

There should be no such thing

There should be no such thing as prisons. What are they thinking? No one commits a crime because their head's all there, except maybe greedy fraudsters and other criminals-on-paper. The people we usually call criminals need our help - for the beatings they took as a child, the molestations they suffered, the body chemistry that has gone awry, the isolations, and every other manifestation of what can go wrong for a person that causes them to spend the rest of their life over-compensating in mistaken, unguided ways.

They should be taken to health resorts instead, with good counselors, pampering to make them feel worthwhile again, and all the tools these places normally use to make the corporately stressed and home-wearied feel good again. Because that's what they really need – to feel good again, to have a laugh, to right the wrongs.

In a generation or maybe two of this, perhaps there would be no more learned problems to pass on. Perhaps we would become the society we pretend to be.

One of the great joys

One of the great joys of being manic is being on a shopping spree, and there is no better destination than Lo Wu. Just over the border from Hong Kong, you're no sooner through customs than in a mall of over five floors, where you can spend until your feet are so tired you take-up one of the many offers you get for a foot massage. Electronics, clothes, shoes, crystals, golfing equipment, pirate DVDs and CDs, jewelry, watches, antiques, copies of Old Masters, production-line watercolours, medications, beauty treatments, dentistry, restaurants, fruit and veggies, toys, carpets, curtains, cushions, and just about everything really. Whatever comes from the great factories that spread for a hundred kilometers from Shenzhen to Guanghzhou, you can get twenty metres inside the border. Hong Kongers make the short train trip there, hit the mall, and then head straight back, never really seeing China at all.

Enter with a mind that has no credit limit and the euphoria is unstoppable. Before you even arrive, from the moment you wake, your heart is beating with the anticipation of one more grand shop. Fidgety on the way there, it's easy to get agitated if you miss just one spot in a queue, or fail to make a train that will be repeated by another in just five minutes anyway.

After the two immigration checkpoints, first the Hong Kong and then the Chinese, you hit the cash machine for some Yuan, cheating the limit by using all your cards and making multiple withdrawals. Knowing that even if this treasury runs empty, you can still get more on your credit card inside for an unreasonable commission that you'll too easily accept.

The first thing to buy is a suitcase to stuff all your purchases in. You'll probably buy another one before the days out, but you modestly start with one. But not the small or medium or large, you get the extra large, the biggest you've got please.

Clothes are good to get at the start because they're light. With them out of the way, it's time for all the random stuff, anything that catches your eye, anything you think is so cheap here that you'll surely be able to get your money back if the day should come that you run out of dough. Grab an antique statue, or another MP3 player, or a remote control helicopter.

Pirate DVDs are left for last, because they make-up the motherload. You sit at a computer screen and select the ones you want, then they call the numbers into a two-way radio, and soon a square of the ceiling is pulled aside and down floods every episode of every TV show you've ever seen and even slightly liked, every Academy Award-winning film in one boxed set, every new release that hasn't even been released yet, every boxed set of every director you've ever admired even one film of. When you get so many that you're onto that second suitcase you start to hope they don't stop you as you pass through customs, but you're invincible, so any concern is fleeting.

Even when you sit down for that foot massage the pace is maintained. May as well get a manicure and pedicure as well, and here comes a lady with a machine that burns off any blemishes; medically questionable and safety notwithstanding, let's have that smell of my own burning flesh.

Time for food. And here is where yum cha finds its true value. It's perfect for manic depressives, with trolley after trolley of different dishes coming around. It's like shopping without having to leave your seat.

The trip home is awkward with weight and too big bags through too thin turnstiles. But the buzz is still there, as you anxiously anticipate pouring the contents of your new bags onto your bed and arranging all you've just purchased into lovely neat self-satisfied categories. It can take months before you wear anything that doesn't need the label ripped-off first.

We go to a discount supermarket

We go to a discount supermarket where they do all sorts of things to make things cheaper. You pay for shopping bags, the aisles aren't that wide, but they're not uncomfortably narrow either. And they don't have to be, because there's just one of everything. There aren't choices upon choices. You want peanut butter – there's one peanut butter, one chocolate, one tomato. Research has been done that shows the more choices you give someone the less happy they are. I never leave our supermarket unhappy.

The best thing of all though, the real buzz, is they have so few staff that there are only ever two checkouts open. But manning these aren't any ordinary checkout dudes, these are guns. Remember there are no bags, unless you buy them, and you have to do the packing yourself afterwards. All these hired hands will do is whisk the items across the reader, and it's up to you to get them from the small counter to the shopping trolley before they start falling over. It's a great sport because that counter is really small, maybe only big enough to hold a packet of cereal and a litre of milk. So they're shooting and you're catching and throwing, catching and throwing.

Lately I've added a level of difficulty. I stack the items on the conveyor belt in the way that is going to make packing afterwards easier. Cold things with cold things, fruits with vegetables, toiletries with cleaning products, soft things and things that will break on top, just like the service assistants pack them in those big plush confusing supermarkets.

The dudes are getting to know me and they smile after a particularly fast shootout, their hands against mine. And I think they've started to notice the professional packing. I swear just today the guy gave me one of those little smirks and nods of acknowledgement you'd only give to a man who can shoot a two dollar coin into the slot of a shopping trolley, then pull it out and wheel it away without even breaking stride.

The most expensive thing in the world

The most expensive thing in the world is convenience. It's the cost of a busy job that consumes more time than is right. When I breakdown what I used to spend on convenience it's frightening. Eating out, buying everything from department stores, 5-star holidays because I didn't have time and wanted to maximize my breaks. And when you work hard you reward yourself expensively. Bargains are for people with time. And better still, the less you pay the greater your sense of achievement.

Parking is a premium

Parking is a premium where we live. Lately there have been a lot of workmen in our building renovating the other apartments, and with their various vans the parking has gotten worse. So there's no more looking for a space that isn't under one of the giant fig trees where the fruit bats rest at night and shit over everything underneath. You just take what you can get.

That bat shit can really burn the paint. You've got to get to it early, or make sure the car has so much polish on it that there's no way the acid can get through. But the bats are beautiful. They sweep over the harbour at dusk and hang like neatly folded umbrellas from the branches just outside our windows. If only they were umbrellas, then they'd catch their own shit. But how nice to be reminded that we're not alone in the city, scratching off love marks in the morning.

Salt dried on the skin

Salt dried on the skin
Somehow sweet to taste
Feeling delicious from the ocean
Bitterness washed away
When do you ever regret a swim?

I have a collection

I have a collection of Chairman Mao statues. My favourite is Mao standing casually with a coat slung over one arm and a cigarette between his fingers. Man of the People. I got him from a wonderful woman who owns a small collectables shop in a side alley in Hong Kong. She could always see me coming. I bought so many Maos off her she called me Chairman Pang, which is as close to the English version of my surname as you're going to get in Chinese. She'd be pulling out all sorts of things to part me with my cash, in a game we both knew we were playing – vases, statues, old Chinese newspapers. I got a fantastic book of Chinese generals once, grim photos with their titles underneath, concertinaed between faded military green silk covers.

She had a wonderful story, having started out as a street hawker selling her wares off a sheet of plastic; she built the business little by little until taking possession of this tiny shop. I knew all this because of a newspaper story she had cut-out, laminated and pinned to the shop wall. Whenever I had spare time and was in the area I would go and visit her, never leaving empty handed.

As a child I used to collect stamps – a magical escape to places I could only dream about. Their foreign alphabets, exotic scenes and unfamiliar portraits were little snapshots of a life I could only imagine. It would be cute to suggest they were the inspiration for later travels, but they weren't, it wasn't even a consideration. I would get them in cheap bagfuls from stationery departments mostly. The more colourful the better. I'd soak the stamps off the remainders of envelopes, let them dry on tea towels, then lovingly place them in my treasured albums, creating impressionistic pages more concerned with the overall effect than any correct ordering.

The best stamps I ever got were from a heavily-accented German builder. I'd worked with him to put the extension on our house. It only took a few weekends and I worked side-by-side with him, giving my best. When we put on the aluminium roof it was torturous, the summer sun reflecting back at us, until I collapsed after lunch with sunstroke. When the job was done he bought me a folder with German and American stamps from WWII. The German ones were mostly of Hitler. The American ones were all of the same size and horizontal in format, and came in identical shades of blue and green, with some red and brown. The way I set the blue and green ones in the album you could blur your eyes and almost see the ocean.

I was deeply touched by this gift. And looking back I am even more touched. Here was a man old enough to have perhaps been in the war, and he gave me a part of his memories. And I still don't know why he chose me, as I didn't even mention my stamps and they were closely hidden away. I stopped collecting not long after that. I'm not sure why, perhaps I felt those pages of American stamps were the best I was ever going to get.

The only other thing I have actively gone out to gather and keep is art. Mostly Chinese watercolours, but also other things that have a watercoloury-feel, such as a photo of a galloping horse taken from the front and intentionally out of focus to capture the movement, and some Henry Miller lithographs from his later years. I have an abundant collection of long horizontal Chinese scrolls, which you gradually roll out and read like a book. They're mostly around fifteen feet long and only a foot or so high. Collecting these has led me up back alleys and into strangers' apartments where anything could have happened to me, but nothing ever has, except excited languageless exchanges, when I have hoped the seller has been at least a little pleased with my interest as much as with their earnings.

Looking back it is perhaps the collecting that's the thing and not the collections themselves. And every day that Mao makes me smile. How wonderful to be so self-important you have to remind people you're ordinary.

Every time we got on that ferry

Every time we got on that ferry it was another throw of the dice. It was an hour of calm before the storm, whisking us from Hong Kong to the Asian gambling Mecca of Macau to meet with one of Las Vegas' royalty, who was setting-up shop there for the first time. I have met royalty of the Middle East, the sheiks born to lead, overseas educated, oil rich, calm in their abundance and certainty of rule. But this was another beast altogether, not quite rising from the street, but definitely from the Strip; where opportunity is equal and unfettered democracy breeds wise-guy rulers with no license for tomorrow. Our guy had given himself the symbols of a cultured rule, but it turned out everything was leased.

On the way my boss would busy himself on his laptop, limbering-up with gymnastic dexterity. I tried to relax, knowing the show was going to see me limp on the return journey. No meeting went for less than seven hours and never without hiccup. Once we were fired and hired again three times in the one meeting. We soon learned the trick – prepare a hundred percent of everything that you could possibly know, with the understanding that you'd only get out five percent. But which five percent? The more we knew the shorter our odds. We were getting the hang of this world.

Another trick is to understand your opponent's mind. At first we would do what was agreed at the end of the last meeting, and then present it at the next. But this was never enough. You had to do what was agreed then think about what might be the next step, and present that. He was counting the deck.

One time he had me locked in an ideas session, one-on-one, bouncing our thoughts back and forth as if the rest of the room wasn't there – not my boss nor the dozen minders that always seemed to accompany him – and I stopped him dead in his tracks. "I like it", I said about one of his ideas, "But where's it going to?" He looked up for the first time to address the room. One by one he scanned each person sitting at the oval table, slowly spelling out his sentence, "Did – you – hear – what – he – just – said – to – me?" Here it comes we all thought, one of his famous table-slamming rants. "From now on I want everyone to ask that question." A combined relief rippled-out in one collective breathe. Sometimes you win.

It went on that way until the new place was open. We left the table with our fee and a lot more. It forged a bond between my boss and I, brothers-in-arms. We learned a lot. Our opponent had forced us to. And not just about him, but about the whole business of gambling, as well as where we were and who we were dealing with and what the future would hold.

I wonder at the hope people bring to casinos. On the land border crossing between Macau and China you can see those coming-in queued and bouncing on their toes in anticipation of the fortunes they will make. On the opposite queues, those returning home barely raise their heads. Look at the places - they can afford giant musical water fountains, entrances the size of football fields, marble as far as you can see – who do the gamblers, think is paying for all that? It's you dummy.

Legal cases

Legal cases are a bit of a bi-polar specialty. It's the lure of a grand pay-off, the buzz of revenge, the imagined stage drama of the courtroom. We're used to excitement, and what better trigger than a good juicy case to set the world to rights? It got that I never left agencies, I just sued them.

The scariest thing I ever did was to go into a chairman's office and rifle through his paperwork to find my evidence. It was there all right. I knew it would be. But my heart was pounding, my stomach churning. What if I got caught? It was genuinely scary. I'd never done anything like that before. It felt somehow criminal. I whisked the offending document away, made copies, then returned it.

The mediation day was very bi-polar appealing. I'd gone to work in the morning unshaven and looking like crap. Then before the meeting I went home, showered and shaved, and put on the new $2,000 suit I'd bought especially for the occasion. The room was magnificently lawyerly with dark woods and floor-to-ceiling windows looking down and out to an endless view. I made sure I stood by the windows. When the agency reps walked in there was obvious shock at my transformation from the morning. And what fun I had after the preliminaries, when I slid three copies of the offending document across the meeting room table. One for the MD, one for the Financial Director, and one for their lawyer. They quickly scurried from the room to phone the chairman, then sulked back in to negotiate the deal they had been told to make. There were threats about how I got the document, but I knew I was in the clear. No one had ever told me not to go into the chairman's office, it wasn't out of bounds, and the evidence was unquestionable. Still, the almost panic I felt when hunting for the document was there, and I probably didn't do as good a deal as I could have.

Within 24 hours I was out of my apartment, checked-in to a motel, and out of the country within three days. None of this panic was necessary, but my mania had been triggered and I was off. I barely left the motel room, happy to watch videos and self-medicate with drink. I'm glad I did it that way. Who knows what sort of harm I might have caused myself otherwise?

I don't have to think very hard to come-up with a long list of times I dodged a bullet like this or by other means. How I managed to avoid the big meltdown for so long is a bit beyond me. And even that I survived. Plus I've learned how to never go there again. So here I am, proof positive of I don't know what. I don't believe in luck or miracles, or some greater fate that awaits. I just figure nature makes it harder to die than you'd think.

Why do candles cry?

Why do candles cry, leaving tears down their clean pillar of promises? Perhaps when we go to sleep they realize their time has come, while we will wake tomorrow.

It is common

It is common among people with mental health issues to struggle with Perfectionism. One of the biggest issues is that it actually stops you from doing things in case you can't do them just right. All day you hear the voice that tells you you're not good enough, forgetting all the things you have succeeded at. The key is to remember what you have done, and done well, and even times when you have helped someone else. I must keep reminding myself that I am not a bad person, better still, that I am ordinary.

There is no such thing

There is no such thing as a time machine and there never will be. If such a thing ever existed then we'd know about it - someone would have come back to us or forward to us. Once a time machine is made in any time it exists for all time. That's just the way it is.

Anthony Peck

I've been thinking

I've been thinking about Time, and especially in relation to how long we have been around as civilizations. Nearing fifty years of age, I have developed that as a unit of time. And fifty doesn't seem very long at all. Only yesterday I was looking up at the kitchen cupboards and wondering when I would be big enough to reach them. So if 50 is a thinkable unit, and it seems so desperately short, then 100 isn't much more – just 2 x 50, or 2 x a very short time.

Now where does 10 times fifty take us? The Renaissance. 10 times something is never very much. If you have 1 orange that's fine, but having 10 oranges doesn't make you that much happier. So the Rennaisance isn't really that long ago.

BC is 40 x 50, or 40 short lives ago. That just doesn't seem much either. And yet we have history books filled with revolutions in thinking and seemingly Teutonic shifts in everyday life during the period since then. So we're really very fickle, jumping around at breakneck speed while rocks stay still and the aboriginal people of Australia haven't changed for 1,200 x 50, except for what we've done to them in the last 4 x 50.

I know this all sounds like it's getting complicated, but pause for a moment and see if you can feel 50 as a time you can comprehend in a meaningful way, and when you've got a feeling for it in your mind and in your bones, then start making the comparisons, doing the math, and perhaps you will see the point. It's just something I've been thinking.

Direct TV Commercials

Direct TV Commercials are those ones that go for two minutes or more and sell things you know you don't want or need the very first time you see them. But the science behind them is undeniable. Basically, if you last longer than ninety seconds watching them, your chances of purchasing are exponentially increased. And since they play them so often, and you feel that you're immune, you stop switching channels when they come on. But then there you are – you've been watching for more than ninety seconds, and now that special space age cleaning cloth is starting to make sense. Sure it does the same job as any other cloth you have, but you're starting to perceive a difference, and that perceived difference may well be worth the sixty dollars they're charging for it. "All you've got to do is pick-up the phone." And this is the point when they cut to a shot of a phone being picked-up. As if saying it isn't enough, you actually have to be shown. The number comes up on the screen now, as well as the acceptable credit cards, which appear as clearly recognizable logos. Of course they accept any credit card – they want your money. But seeing the logo of your credit card rewards you for having a card that works. It says that you are a respectable part of the community, your credit is good, you can have this or anything else you want. And what's sixty dollars when your family can be protected from all those germs in your house – in the bathroom, the kitchen, right where your children go to sleep!? Go online now or call this number. And though we're going to play this commercial again in fifteen minutes, there's a limited number available. Our operators are standing-by. They're not sitting lazily, they're standing, and they're on their tippy-toes just waiting for your call. Act now and we'll double the offer. No, we'll triple it. You won't just be buying for yourself; you'll also be able to give these cloths away to those you really care about. Remember those germs – they're everywhere.

The latest craze in Direct TVCs is for Funeral Cover. They've skipped the germs and now we're all going to die. Call now!

I find myself

I find myself not saying the obvious jokes a space has been made for. Or the supporting fact nobody needs. Or that anecdote that says I understand just what you mean. Or the disguised boast that uses the current subject for its wedge. I am learning to hold my tongue, and feel much better for the relief.

Things you can't hide

Boredom
Tiredness
Deceit
Stains
Delight
Disapproval
Anger
Ignorance
Prejudice
Struggle
Shyness
Longing
Age
Youth

Sometimes it's just easier

Sometimes it's just easier to take another anti-psychotic pill than try to use all the new techniques I've learned to get a manic state under control. Don't get me wrong, all those techniques are useful and work, but when you feel like it's just running-away and it's scary to think of where it may lead, then a pill and a lie-down seems a valid solution.

At least at those times I've been aware enough to know I need to do something, and I wouldn't have that awareness without the learning's. It can be a strange feeling: an aching in the chest, a light head, a constant leaping to what's next, what's next? Also a feeling of failure, like I thought I had this under control but the bastard's getting away again. But don't go there, because that's igniting it in another way - the failure thing, the unrealistic expectations, the perfectionism that is a constant pusher of negative thinking that will only send me spiraling up and up.

It's got me now, but I'm still aware and holding on. It's not a failure, but I'm going to reach for that extra pill, dinner, and then bed.

I could write this all night, but I won't. Just a little more, to say that this has been going for a few weeks now and some of it has been good and I've been able to 'ride the high'. But this is the second time I'm reaching for the extra meds, like I did yesterday, and it's not feeling good.

Not everything

Not everything is a product. Some things are just done for the doing and better left that way. Some people can't help but turn the well-crafted into a profit. They're the ones who go into businesses, not out of a passion, but because they think they will turn a buck, any buck. There is strangeness to these people - always greedy, always with a motive. Commonly they talk at you, pushing every point home. They scare me with a vision of the world that is never simply beautiful or true.

I've worked it out

I've worked it out – the news programmes have amnesia. It all makes sense. Night after night, they show stories barely different from those the night before. All that seriousness reminds you of the truism that the best comedy is done straight. I correct myself with the knowledge that what's reported is happening to real people and I should be ashamed of my flippancy. I cannot hide behind percentages and say these stories are trivial. Nor can I be callow and suggest more good news should be delivered; that would just be wet. But amnesia - there's an explanation I can live with.

Cigarettes are bad for you

Cigarettes are bad for you, but are soothing as you feel the smoke drawn through. Many people with bi-polar and other mental illnesses like to smoke. It's said it is their need for calm. Those few minutes of quiet reflection as all else is put to one side and the brain gets relief and you simply breathe.

If you're on certain medications there's also a lovely feeling that is more intense than the usual Smokey drag. The best comparison is probably the sensation of smoking while drinking kava. Even people who don't smoke usually do when they have kava. It's the drink of the South Pacific, made from the roots of the same-named plant.

One of the great places for Kava is Vanuatu. You drive along bumpy country roads in the dark until you come to a post with a candle burning on it, which is a sign that kava is available there that night. Then you go through a gate and travel even deeper into the country, jolting along in a utility truck, up and down grassy mounds until you come to a shed where kava is served from a booth made of chicken wire.

There are two sizes of cup to choose from, and you can only buy individual cigarettes, which are laid-out in neat rows on the counter. The kava is like mud, and soon after you drink you start spitting to get rid of the excess saliva that it encourages. Your lips and tongue go numb. The idea of the cigarette is to inhale, and then as you exhale, let your spirit fly out with the smoke, and watch as it wanders into the sky. All is next to silent in the shed under the stars where men only sit, spit and follow their drifting souls.

You need to be very careful about just how much kava you have, as the next morning it can be very difficult to get out of bed, your muscles not responding to the commands your brain tries to send. Perhaps it's because your spirit is having trouble finding its way back into your body.

It doesn't last

It doesn't last, that sweet almost-puffiness of your loved. Scientifically it's probably got something to do with muscles relaxing in sleep or whatever. But it's not science you see. Instead the full sweetness of her delicious face caught in the gauze of morning light. It's then you want to hold back the day for one more luscious bite.

Things that you do but don't know if they work

Vitamins
Crystals
Diets
Car tune-ups
After shave
Detoxing
Eating carrots
Punctuality

A long drive

A long drive helps you get out the kinks. Sure you may end-up with a stiff neck, but that's not the sort of kink it fixes. It's a meditation thing when you're doing it on your own. Each white spaced line a pulse, even more hypnotic in the night when there are no distractions. Thoughts come, thoughts go. There's enough to concentrate on with the driving to never get too caught up on one thing. There's also the motion of always going forward. Your thoughts head that way too; because you're obviously going somewhere, and usually somewhere you're excited about if it's a long drive.

As a couple it can be its own balm. There are things you've left unsaid that now have the space to be spoken. It's not so much that you have a captive audience, but that you now have an uninterrupted chance to share. And that includes the silences. You know you're doing alright when you can be quiet together and not feel the need to fill the gaps.

A familiar long drive is the best. Knowing what to expect, the driving doing itself, no anxiety about when you will arrive - there's nothing left but this moment. The Buddha probably would have made a great long-haul truckie.

I know it's dangerous

I know it's dangerous, but hitch-hiking is really fun. And I know it's a very bi-polar thing to do, because it's assumes invincibility, and I know the times I've done it I have been in a manic phase, but really it is a great thing. You get to see the world very differently. And not just because of the variety of people who stop and give you a ride, and the out of the way detours it takes you on, but for the times when you're not in a car and you're just walking, in the middle of nowhere, on a road that is usually driven and rarely walked.

One time I was on a road that hardly anyone drove along. In fact I had sort of given-up on anyone coming by, and had settled into walking as far as I had to before reaching the next town, which was probably another 50 kilometres away. The ocean was to my left, but with the view blocked by grassed-over dunes and too far away for me to hear the sound of waves. On the right was just scrub. What struck me most was how much life there was. Crabs scurried, ants marched in columns, insects jumped or rushed about, lizards darted, snakes swished through grasses. You'd think I was in the middle of nowhere and all alone, but that was far from the truth. The guy who eventually picked me up said he didn't want to stop for me, but he figured I would be stuck otherwise. I didn't feel stuck at all, but was glad enough for the ride.

Vinyl is best

Vinyl is best for a number of reasons. Firstly, it is better than digital because digital only records sound. There has to be something there for digital to put down a one or a zero. Vinyl records silence. And as there is no absolute silence in a recording studio, then that's quite a lot it picks-up. And we're not talking about people fumbling over drumsticks or fidgeting with microphones, but the atmosphere, the very air in the room. And who is to say that this atmosphere isn't part of the song? And perhaps even is somehow an amplifier for unsounded feelings? Though this last is probably going too far.

The other advantage of vinyl is you're more likely to hear the music as it sounded when it was recorded. This is particularly so with older music. How much more authentic to hear it as it was heard the first time, mum and dad putting the album on the turntable of their stereograph with a crackle, a hiss? And that is how you will always warmly remember those songs - not awkwardly wedged in your ears with the 8:15 screeching into the station and wondering if you'll get a seat.

The most luxurious thing

The most luxurious thing is to not work. Not that working is bad - we were made to work, ever since people have existed and needed to eat. It's one of the things that make us what we are. But not working, even on the weekend, what bliss. That Saturday morning feeling with no timetable - a little longer in bed, a little more breakfast, things to do in your own good time.

A long period of not working, if you are free of the anxiety of how you're going to manage, is double happiness. It takes some time to get used to, but once surrendered you see how much more there is. Waves to watch, breezes to feel, colours to soak in, conversations to be prolonged, people to be enjoyed, talents to be played with, every emotion of sky - angry when thundering, busily windy, restfully still in the eye of a storm.

Without leaving your home it's amazing how much life goes on independently of any demands you might make of yourself or the world. A trail of ants, a cockroach, birds, worms just beneath the surface, busy centipedes. Check-in on plants every day and you'll see they're up to their own thing - sprouting bits, turning to the sun, stretching roots. Time doesn't equal money after all.

Who cares?

Who cares what the government does? There is so much out of their control it's a wonder we bother. They even remind us of this fact. "Don't blame us," they say, "the economy is down because of market forces." Or, "We can't spend the money improving transport, because nobody wants to use it."

Yet we persist, and not in any rational way, but like supporting a sports team. You pick your side and stick with them for life. Election counts are run like a scoreboard. Even without knowing who a player is we can pick which team they're on from the material and cut of their suit or outfit. Parliaments are run with a referee who sits at a high table, looking down to see that no one breaks the rules. Interviews are rolled out with the same predictable platitudes or accusations rehearsed by players and coaches under the guidance of media trainers. "It wasn't just me out there, it was a team effort, I'd like to thank all the boys." Polls are marched out like game stats.

Has everyone forgotten what government is for? Not for those figures that can be changed out on a board, but for those things that don't produce figures. Government doesn't exist to make a profit or score a goal. It's there for the things that business won't touch. Not for the fickle scorecard, but for how the game is played.

We're a lucky generation

We're a lucky generation, having never been to war. Certainly there are wars everywhere at the moment, but our generation has managed to skip them. The last conscripted war we were in was Vietnam, and even that was a lottery as to whether you got sent or not. In our house we grew up with the fear of that war. As children our parents scared the hell out of us thinking that when we came of age there would be full conscription. We were pushed for good grades so we could at least go to uni to avoid it, or at worst be made officers and hopefully be further back in the lines. They themselves had gotten off scott-free, just babes during the Second World War. But they talked about it like they were in it, and it didn't help that our history books were full of that war and documentaries about it peppered our TV screens.

War hung so heavily over us that even now I wonder what it would be like – the noise of guns and low flying planes overhead, the fear of leaving the trench to almost certain death, the burn of metal in flesh, maybe coming home without an eye or a leg. There's even a perverse part of me, in a time when we get to experience so much, with travel so cheap and opportunities so open, that regrets missing out on this greatest of tests. Wanting to know the limits of what can be endured. Am I made of the Right Stuff? I momentarily forget that the premise of fighting in a war is to kill people. It's that thought which stops me cold. How would I go killing someone else?

Right now there's a guy using one of those garden blowers outside the window, and I'm wishing they would opt for the silence of a broom instead. But I'll probably get over it. So how far am I really prepared to go?

It's been a slow starting year

It's been a slow starting year, so slow I was able to buy a $70 page-a-day diary for $6 I got it so late. I think that was in June. Black faux-leather covers, address book, planners, colour maps. The first entry wasn't until July, for a doctor's appointment. Even after that there are few markings, weeks and weeks going blank. You'd wonder why I should want such a grand diary, but it was so cheap, and who is to say it wasn't a grand year after all?

Numbers seem to matter

Numbers seem to matter far too much to me. I'm not blaming anyone else but myself. I 'Select All' on the computer screen and use 'Tools' to get a 'Word Count'. Work goals are set in numbers of days. Today I will write two thousand words. I will go in the water for two hours. My exercise routine will be for fifty minutes. Yesterday it was for forty-five. I have lived in over forty homes, had over twenty jobs, and lived in nine cities on four continents.

Somehow I have digitized myself.

There's a form

There's a form for everything these days. You can't do anything without filling one out. And you always go away with a copy that you're going to throw out anyway.

In the bathroom

In the bathroom of the house I grew-up in, the tiles had a speckled pattern. I remember sitting on the toilet and being able to make out an image of 'The Cat in the Hat' in them. That was years ago. I remember every time I fixed my eyes on that patterned image it surprised me, as if I was seeing it for the first time. And I remember being delighted all over again.

Anthony Peck

The giving of gifts

The giving of gifts has always been important to me. Knowing what I now do about bi-polar, some of the shine on my seeming generosity has been dusted off. It's a common symptom. But at least one that's hard to regret.

When I was young I received a small amount of pocket money, which I never spent at the time. I saved it for two things: our annual holiday to the beach, and Christmas presents. Fortunately the holiday was in May, so it was a more or less 50/50 split.

On a day I had been looking forward to for half a year, I would walk up the hill to the local mall, and in no time at all would be happily making my way home again with my purchases. It was always easy to buy something I thought appropriate for each person. They weren't extravagant things – bath salts, a book, crayons – but they were all a treat, steering clear of anything practical. It gave me so much pleasure to do the buying, and I wrapped them with equal care, attaching little cards that I tried to personalize as much as seasonal clichés would allow.

On Christmas Day I was more interested in other's delight than caring what I received from them. In a way I was trained not to expect much. The worst blow was the Christmas I received a scooter that snapped right across the standing board on the first hill I attempted. And it was such a beautifully shiny new thing. It was never replaced and I just went back to my brother's old one. 'Second Hand Rose' my father would call me. I learned not to mind; learned very early so that I can never remember being resistant in any way. The thought of being disappointed never crossed my mind, which seems strange in retrospect. Even now there is much I could say on the topic, but will easily refrain.

I have made ridiculous gestures over the years. Often shouting the whole bar, or buying some outrageously expensive gift, or making sure every single person I know has gotten something truly special for them at Christmas. For someone with bi-polar it's a double delight, not only do you get to feed your appetite for generosity, you get to shop.

The gifts I get embarrass in a way that is out of proportion. I find it almost hurtful to receive. Perhaps it's in anticipation of getting another broken scooter, too cheap to hold the weight of a six year old.

Anthony Peck

Who will ever forget?

Who will ever forget their first bike? In our family you received it on your thirteenth birthday. Mine had 28-inch wheels, a dragster seat, and hub gears. It was a second-hand bike and the gears were busted, but that didn't matter. I think they were locked in third gear and that got my legs strong quickly. Every now and then the gear would slip under pressure, which did my nuts all sorts of damage as I'd slam down hard on the cross-bar. But that never bothered me too much. It was a bike and it was freedom.

I never rode with anyone. My brothers are three years older and were busy doing their own things. And we never got to know the other neighbourhood kids because we went to school so far away. I'd just get on my bike on the weekends and ride. Sometimes I'd visit friends who lived suburbs away. That was before mobile phones, and when you didn't bother ringing ahead anyway. They were there or they weren't. And if they were busy they'd tell you and off you'd go. I got brave and started to ride into the city. And when I couldn't sleep at night, which was most nights, I'd sneak my bike out of the garage and ride the empty streets for hours.

When I left home I bought myself a new bike – 10-speeds, with racing handlebars. It was still second-hand, but a quantum leap from what I had been riding. Each weekday I rode it to where I worked in a government office in the city, then home, then off to uni where I studied at night, then home again from there.

There was a local bike shop near where I lived that I used to visit so often I'm sure the guy who owned it got sick of me. Then one day he told me about a new racing bike that was coming out and that would be quite cheap for what it was. I bought the first one he got in. It was beautiful. Silver, lightweight, quality Shimano brakes and gears. You couldn't get me off the thing. My legs became my obsession. I'd just stick them out in front of me and stare down at them. I started to shave them too, as I noticed that's what all the really good riders did.

Instead of studying at night, I switched to days for my second year at uni and got a job as the boy on a milk run. I'd get up at about one o'clock in the morning and cycle across the Harbour Bridge to the milk depot. Then I'd run bottles until seven in the morning, before heading back home for a shower and a quick nap, and then off to uni for the day. I became known at uni for always being with my bike. I'd take it into tutorials with me. If I got a few spare hours I'd head-out for some more riding. I also used to go to the pool and knock off a kilometer. Every day I was riding about fifty kilometers, running eleven and swimming one. I was superfit.

I've written-off about five bikes. Got caught in the back wheel of a turning semi-trailer, stuck under the front of a car that turned onto me, went over the handle-bars at the bottom of a steep hill when I hit some gravel. That last one split my helmet, and I had to get a chiropractor to push my skull back into shape every second day through the roof of my mouth. I still have a bike, but I'm not game enough to get back on yet. Probably best to wait until I'm fully healed.

I have always liked

I have always liked bearish men – not in a poofy way – I just seem to warm to them. Maybe it's their bustling manner – robust, jovial, and welcoming. And fearless, or at least not shy. You know where you stand with them and there is a natural warmth. Things seem effortless for these men, their physical presence suggesting there would be no beating them if you were so foolish as to try and take them on. But not in an aggressive way, they seem like they might choose to joke you to death instead.

Tarek is a fearsome looking gentle giant. Half Egyptian half Scottish, he wears the traditional Middle Eastern goatee. Amazingly he can be fully Scottish and fully Egyptian, depending on the occasion. Watching a rugby game in the pub he is a lad. Haggling over a quote or selling some work he is a camel salesman; with all the gesturing, pleas to heaven, and poetry which Arabic seems uniquely capable of.

I was his senior and used to berate him for not following procedure. I kept insisting that the time had come for him to grow into a more international and world-class operator. And that having a history of success for pulling things off didn't excuse the way other people and the work would had to suffer in the process. Sheepishly and cajolingly he would come into my office and tell me the latest potential for disaster. Trying at first to make it seem normal, but fully prepared to make a defence-cum-plea when I would see through it. But how could I refuse those eyes?

I can proudly say we were a team, which made going to meetings together something we both looked forward to. It was through him that I learned my Arab bargaining ways. "You want us to help you sell your new building. How much for one apartment? A million? So you can see you get a whole campaign for the price of just one of your bathrooms…"

When I was ill he came to see me, putting-up with my dementia, which I'm told included me still lecturing him on why he should do things the normal way. Even then I couldn't let it go. Because I cared for him. Cared so much that I'm smiling now, picturing his face and watching him throw his hands in the air as the winger spills the ball over the line, or a businessman in full dish-dash suggests the price is too high.

Ross is a small bear. Not much taller than me but muscular, and most bearlike for his bustling physicality. And a bear's temper. In one day you couldn't count the times he would get a thorn in his paw. The new company logo at the front of the office would be in the wrong font, or the video conferencing equipment would be faulty – "I thought we were a communications business!?" We sat opposite each other and I could and would listen to these rants all day. They made me smile. It would scare the younger ones and trouble some of our seniors, but mostly they were missing the point. No one was more passionate or cared with greater ferocity than Ross.

As with Tarek, we were partners. But more equally so, working at the same level and equally delighted, frustrated and amused by Hong Kong. He loved Chinglish and would daily site his latest discovery. "Hey look, there's a printers called Fuk Yu." We often lunched together, choosing anything from the local workers' noodle shop to a fully pomped Italian restaurant.

One of our fondest shared memories is the time we were sacked by a client. We went to their office to show them some ideas we'd developed off our own bat. We were being proactive because this client was starting to slip from our grasp. When we'd initially won the account Ross was friends with the boss, but he had gone, then the next layer down had gone, until now an accountant was our most senior contact. She sat us down and we told her we had some fresh ideas for a problem we knew they were having. She interrupted with the news that our services were no longer needed. It was difficult for either of us to keep a straight face. We graciously acknowledged the situation and thanked her for the business to date. In the back of our minds we knew it wouldn't affect our bottom-line as we had plenty of work at that time. As we were leaving she asked if she could see the ideas tucked in our neat black satchel. I declined. As soon as we got in the lift we both burst into laughter. It felt so cool to have refused to show the work. We weren't going to pander, we were professionals. It fed right into Ross' vision of how a business should be.

My uncle Gary is my biggest bear of all. Not physically as big as Tarek, but not much short of it either. His stature comes from within. Not my uncle by blood, but my mother's sister's husband. Nevertheless I feel tied to him as strong as any genealogical bond could be. And I know I'm not alone in this. There are many people who rate Gary's influence on them as one of their strongest. He is the mentor-of-all. And every contact with him is another step in your Programme.

Fully conscience of his affect, he has jokingly developed a hierarchy: you start as a Student, and then move to Teacher, then Guru, and finally Oracle. He's recently given himself Oracle status. He works on his confidence with constant self-referencing that can come-off to the uninitiated as brashness. But for us disciples he works on building our confidence even more than his own. In public this coaxing is usually delivered in negative terms. We are all "boofheads" and "nancy-boys", who if are not careful will be "voted off the team". Privately the support you receive is couched lovingly, concernedly, knowledgeably, generously. It is then that the bear has you in his hug.

And you can't fault his experience. If I ever have a problem I just tell him, and in very simple terms he will provide a solution that is obvious and correct, yet always surprising. You know you could never have come up with it yourself, but you also know automatically that it's right.

And there is a secret behind all this wisdom and caring – Mama Bear. My Aunty Jan is the usually quiet voice in what is a true partnership. Mysteriously her presence is somehow present in all the wise advice. When you visit them the cave is always warm inside and the porridge waiting on the table.

The first time Jerry and I met it was kismet. We thought the same, used the same language, laughed at the same things. He's the bear you can have a friendly wrestle with. Though my senior in work, he treats me as an equal. And he is my friend. He was the first to call when I lay in hospital. There was only one thing he wanted - to know what I wanted. He uttered those magical words, "If there's anything you need, anything at all..."

I have seen him brilliant in meetings, withering in corrections, wise in recommendations. We have both had our troubles and both seen them through. Acknowledging our regrets, we can look each other easily in the eye when others would avoid the truths we've learned.

Mark is a bear of the same height as me, but more muscular in build. He is my best friend, though we go for years without seeing each other and months without talking. He has lived more than half his life overseas, but it is the time we shared together back home in our youth that has mattered and sustained our friendship. He is a bustling-bear of the Ross type. A highly qualified and respected intellectual, he can turn from raging at the wrongs of the world to being beer-guzzlingly obnoxious. The later is one of his most endearing traits, though it's hard to explain that to some people. We have been drunk together too many times to recount. And the stories of these episodes are still recalled today by those who were present and some who weren't. Though we, of course, have little memory.

One of my treasures is a tape I still have from an old answering phone we had when we once lived together. Almost every message is a sozzled plea from one of us to the other begging to be let into the apartment at around five in the morning, because we'd lost our key again.

I was his boss once at a niteclub, where he cooked in the downstairs restaurant until it was time to open the bar. I had to let him go in the end because we were both getting too pissed to run the show, and the owner insisted. But overall we looked after each other. There was a day I yelled him back to life after he'd lost his way with an understandable grief. While he would tolerate my naked performances of Gigi, delivered from the bathtub, with one leg high-kicking over its edge. But it was always effortless to be together, despite the sometimes pain we both experienced.

The other day we were talking on the phone and I was explaining a bit about bi-polar by reminding him how he always used to say I was more normal after a few drinks. It hurts that I haven't seen him since it all happened. In his voice I can tell he's searching back for signs he should have picked-up or wondering mistakenly if he failed in any way. I just want to take him in my arms and squeeze him, and by osmosis have him lose any doubts, and discount nothing of what we've shared or been to each other. I want it to be my turn to be the bear.

I can imagine me and my furry men sitting by a campfire; me happiest for having them all together at once. We would share stories unlike any men's group huddled in a Smokey confessional tent, passing a talking stick. Ours is the outdoors, the world, and all the fun to be had in it.

Camping

Camping is the best holiday. Hotels suck. You never meet anyone and the places are all the same. If you do try to be friendly to people it can come across as creepy. But camping in a caravan park forces you to meet people. They're at the barbeque, in the amenities block, parked right beside you with just canvas separating. And caravan parks tend to be in the best places – right on the beach or by a river. You're part of a fraternity, and people are nice to each other and help each other out.

Camping also gets you closer to nature, because it's right there. The wind makes your walls flap, the sounds of leaves rustling or waves breaking are your soundtrack. You're forced to a basic way of living, which is a huge relief after always having to make sure the carpets are vacuumed, and the lights are switched off, the doors locked, the cushions fluffed, and all those things that just seem like must-dos within solid walls. When camping you realize how little you really have to do to be comfortable, because you adjust what you think of as being comfortable in the first place. The moment you decide to have a camping trip you're automatically free.

When you camp in National Parks and other free-range campsites, you feel freest of all. You don't even have to check-in, a bubbling creek is your amenities block, and the shop is whatever you brought in your esky.

I was never an alter boy

I was never an alter boy, though I would have liked to have been. I don't know what they do now, but back then you wore a red cloak over a white surplice with a red robe underneath. Angelic. I have seen better since, at Sacré Coeur on Christmas Day. I counted fourteen rows of alter boys and girls all in white, from top to toe. High up in the viewing area, with the light streaming down as if through clouds like the glow of god, it was truly otherworldy, stage-managed for inspiration.

The moment I found out I was not to be an alter boy was unpleasant. The local parish priest had made a rare appearance at school assembly and announced our entire year would train for the honour. He then left the stage and walked straight to me. "You won't be joining the other boys. Your brothers haven't been able to serve during the week because they go to school so far away, and since you'll be going to the same school next year I've decided not to make you an alter boy." It wasn't a private announcement but a very public proclamation, and there was vitriol in it. He was of the 'Hell and Damnation' school and his sermons were an exercise in terror. We by far preferred the junior priest, who was once clocked delivering a sermon in under two minutes. You remembered more from his few words than from the full half-hour of frothy spray that would spit from his more senior Servant of God.

One time the pope was visiting our city and was heading to a museum where a crowd of people awaited. I was walking along the footpath, further up the street, with no one else in sight and all traffic cleared. So for a moment it was just me and the pope in his special white pope-mobile with the bullet glass and the mounted throne. I stopped and looked at him, he looked at me, we both waved. It was memorable because of how casual it was, how free of the pomp I had admired and looked up to as a child, but which was denied me. It didn't seem to matter that I hadn't been an alter boy. And besides, by then the pope was just another bloke to me.

Having a heightened sense

Having a heightened sense of things spiritual joins the list of bi-polar traits. We think we have knowledge denied the rest of the world, a special connection with the universe. You say things that could get you locked-up. I didn't suffer that fate, but boy did I push it.

It began with my discovery of rebirthing. You lie on your back and breathe in and out without pause. After a few minutes you start to tingle in different parts of your body. Before you know it some parts begin to go into cramped paralysis. A memory flashes into your mind, your body often convulses, and then you can be either crying or laughing uncontrollably. You keep breathing through it, reliving your memory so vividly it's as if you're experiencing it fully for the first time. When it's over the feeling of relaxation is immense. It's as if you've had that part of your brain that was troubling you removed, never needing to go over it again, not even wanting to talk about it. It's quite simply gone.

I had been working with one particular rebirther for some time. A very warm and caring lady who would lead me through the process. It became a weekly thing at a time when I was working in Brisbane. It was a period of great freedom for me. I had arranged to work just three days a week in the city, and then would drive south to the beach for four days, setting-up my combie van almost on the sand. It was the best set-up. I'd had a double bed built into the back of the van, complete with teak bed head, and a map light built into it for reading at night. Underneath the bed were slide rails holding a big metal strongbox containing my phone, computer, printer and sound system. There was also an annexe that attached to the sliding door, providing a tented office overlooking the waves. When the surf was up I surfed. When the surf was flat I worked. Driving around I wore a big headset listening only to the Beach Boys. When I passed another combie I gave the traditional 'Peace' sign.

The rebirthing was helping me to feel great. Perhaps a little too great. I could do anything it seemed. The world was all-beautiful, all-magical, I was at One. So when I was introduced to Breatharianism it seemed to make sense. The idea is based on surrender. You show so much faith in the universe that you place yourself entirely in its care, promising no intervention to provide for your survival. Like a plant you live on air, sunshine and water. The theory is that we know Vitamin D is produced in the body through exposure to the sun, so why not our other nutrients? Breatharians realize that this is not possible in a modern environment where air-conditioning and pollution interfere with the air, living predominantly inside restricts the amount of sunshine we get, and water is filled with impurities. So to practice Breatharianism you need to live fully in nature. I took it all on. But knowing I was part of the modern world and wanted to remain so, I chose just to do it for a short period of time.

My rebirther helped me. She took me to a site in the rainforest that had a rundown lean-to made of bits of corrugated iron, cardboard and discarded wood, with a big fire pit in the middle of a barely supporting wooden platform. Nearby in a clearing of the forest was a metal bathtub, complete with a firepit below and a brick chimney, so you could lay in the bath on a wooden board to stop you getting burnt on the metal, and keep the water warm by feeding the fire. I was supplied with a good load of wood for both the bath and the fire-pit in the lean-to.

To make the transformation to Breatharianism certain steps need to be taken. The first week is nil-by-mouth. You can gargle water but must spit it out. There are only three activities. You meditate on the fire, then bathe away whatever has come up during the meditation, and you sleep. After the first week you can start drinking water.

I never made it to that second week, but the first week had me buzzing. The meditations on the fire were suitably hypnotizing. Nothing greatly traumatic came up; I was feeling invincible. The bathes were long and luxurious, staring up into the canopy without a single care. I kept the fire well stoked and would remain in there for five hours at a time. I needed to sleep less and less. The not eating or drinking didn't bother me. And it was a reward when I'd do a shit and it would come out all green and sticky, proving that my body was being cleansed to the core. My rebirther visited every few days to see that all was well. My relative stillness had the added benefit of encouraging the wildlife around to treat me as one of their own. After a few days they started to come out and visit. I began to feel like a Saint Francis of Assisi.

I don't know what motivated me to re-enter the world, but I was pumped. I went to my van, which was parked nearby on a bushfire track, and slid open the side door, only to have it come off its railing. No worries. I picked up the door like it was made of cardboard and easily slid it back. I had never felt so strong.

I drove a heavenly thousand kilometers that day. And remember looking around as if I could pick-out an individual blade of grass, and not just capture it optically, but reach into its very being and converse with it. It was me and I was it and we were One. I had achieved nirvana and nothing could touch me and all could touch me beautifully.

When I got to Sydney I went to my sister's place. She was preparing for her wedding, and I made sure I became instrumental in the celebration of this great love that symbolized all the Love that is and was and ever will be.

I don't know what brought me down to earth, or when or how it happened. But I rode that high like an airborne charioteer. How I didn't go over the top is a surprise to me now, especially knowing what I do. But as it didn't end unhappily I have no regrets, and can even feel a sneaking pleasure in the indescribable joy my condition once gave me.

Is there a book?

Is there a book
somewhere written
to tell
me how
or write
of me
plainly?

For me
a manual
for friends
an excuse
to take away
their shyness
knowing me.

In eyes
a history
unspoken
frightened
yet insistent
with questions
doubtfully accusing.

I can tell
you
it was me
never you
and memories
cherished
or questioned
are still
ours to share.

You can always

You can always wave at a dog. There'll be a car stopped at the traffic lights with a dog sitting on one of the passenger's laps, and you merrily wave at the dog. Even though you've never met or even seen the dog before, and knowing that it's not going to wave back. And yet you'd never consider simply waving at people you don't know. Though you can wave at children.

I have tried

I have tried and failed and promise never to try again. The movie business is brutal. To begin, the numbers are stacked against you. Thousands of films get made each year and only a few make it to cinema screens. And those that do usually only have short runs of a couple of weeks or so. The next layer down go straight to DVD. The layer below that might make it into an obscure category at a film festival. Below that is playing your life's work on a plasma screen to family and friends. So in a year only a handful of films will break even, let alone turn a profit. But what a profit they make - not just with ticket sales, but DVD sales, merchandising, product placement. The numbers are so boggling that making a film looks like a quick way to earn a buck. Of course you could make it just for art, but then it's guaranteed to really cost you.

A friend and I tried to get a film up. We spent almost five years and about $50,000 each on trips to London and LA and Italy – doing castings, trying to raise distribution deals, attending film markets. We got very close, only to be denied when the investor who had given it the famous 'green light' found he had lost too much money the year before. One day we were about to get on the plane back to LA, the next we were not. That's when we called it quits.

It started out as a good idea. He would direct, I would write. We chose the horror genre, as this seems to be a good way to get in with your first film. He'd always made short horror films anyway; incoherent things that made a poor showreel when we got in front of potential backers. But that's what we had. That and the script. He had a storyline idea upfront and I worked with that. I worked with it through twelve iterations, changing it as we received each new input from the money people. In the end it was barely recognizable from where we had begun. I would set my alarm for 2am, work on it until 7am, then be at my desk by 7.30am to work my usual twelve-hour day. The first draft took six weeks of doing this. Each new iteration then took at least two weeks. And as the drafts came off the printer I'd be close to collapse.

But I never thought of it as asking too much. In fact I never had any real feelings about the project at all. I can't once remember being excited or disappointed. I just did it. It wasn't my thing, it was my friend's. And it's not that I valued this friendship so much that I was joyfully sharing the ride, or was doing it for his sake. It's just that he'd asked me. Back then if anyone asked me to do anything I would do it. I'd break my back at work, find someone a new job, lend money, move house for someone. The list of things I would have to do each day for other people was almost as long as my work list. And not one of these things did I care about. If you asked you got.

In psychological terms they call this 'Subjugation', and it generally comes from being brought up in a way that has you putting other people's interests in front of yours all the time. It's one of the 'Schemas', of which there are eighteen – Perfectionism, Defectiveness, Social Isolation, and so on. Understanding them and fixing them forms part of Cognitive Therapy Treatment (CTT). People with bi-polar tend to have quite a few, and the treating of them is very important, as it helps avoid the thinking and behaviours that can lead to a race up or down. Without this kind of treatment I can't imagine trying to manage the condition. It seems that while someone may be genetically predisposed to bi-polar, it only gets triggered if the person experiences traumas and other stresses that bring it on.

All of this has come as a great relief to me, and my own treatment has been great. I know where I'm at and how and when to pull back as I start to feel the pendulum swing. It's made me think that everyone should have CCT and what a pleasant world it would be if they did. We've all got something. But life is not a movie, and there are few box office hits.

Waiting comes easily

Waiting comes easily to me. I waited a lot as a child, as I think a lot of middle children do. You wait for your elder siblings to finish their things, then once they have moved on, you wait for the younger ones to do theirs. You do a lot of this waiting with mothers, as unfortunately for them they usually provide the transport service. This can be a valuable learning, as you get to see your mother in the context of other people and as a person in her own right. You also learn patience. And this patience becomes almost immediately useful in your first amorous relationships, when you don't have a car and do a lot of waiting at railways stations and bus stops or in front of cinemas or dances.

But this is pure bloody-minded patience and not your ultimate goal. Where you want to really get, is when waiting for someone is treated as your own special time. When you can make the most of what you've crammed into your head all these years. Allowing you to take a pleasant tour through it all. Your friend arrives and you are almost startled they're there, as if it's a chance meeting, and a new chapter to add to your well-furnished mind.

Politics is easy

Politics is easy to spot, it's when someone plays the man and not the ball. Every time you feel like you're being played, you just have to stop and bring it back to the issue.

The trick is to realize it's happening, and that can be difficult because if you're being played it hurts. You've got to get over that, see through it, and say, "No, this is not about me, it's about this issue." The great thing once you've gotten this down pat, is that as soon as you see they're playing you, that's when you've got them on the ropes. They've resorted to the lowest form of argument, which means they've got nothing.

Politicians in business or any other pursuit rise to the top easily. Their only problem is that it just takes another politician to knock them off. If you get to the top using your abilities you stand on a rock solid pyramid of undeniable talent. You will take knocks, but you're never far from scrambling back to the summit you created.

I can be blasé on this topic now, but once it was not so clear and would consume me in a very bi-polar way. I would stew and stew and imagine terrifying revenge. But that's all over now and I can appear most wise after the event. But where else does wisdom come from?

Australia is the only country I know

Australia is the only country I know with a national anthem that doesn't have a Call-to-Arms. Sure it's a bit soppy and we struggle to make sense of it and no one really loves it, but maybe that's a good thing. We don't even know all the words. Maybe it means that being Australian doesn't require a devotion that can turn into something more dangerous. We are comfortable, unthreatened, and hopefully accepting. We have seen waves of immigration, and within a generation or two these new Australians are as like the rest of us as is possible. It means we've largely avoided ghettos.

And yet we are more likely to join in someone else's war than anyone else. If there's a fight on you'll find Australians there. The only time we've had real cause to fight was against the Japanese. The rest is done supposedly for our allies and the promise that if anyone did try to take us, then they would reciprocate.

But plenty of studies have shown, not that we're invincible, but that we're indefensible. Which, despite what that sounds like, might be even better. We're sort of the Afghanistan of the south. Invade us in Sydney and troops can come and push you out from Brisbane or Melbourne. Taken one day, we would be released the next. Unless someone was able to invade all the major cities at once, though this wouldn't work either as troops would simply have to come out of the desert. In the case of atomic strikes on all the major cities, there'd be enough time-lag for retaliation.

I don't know why we have an army at all. Not that I don't admire them for all the humanitarian work they do, it's just we don't really need them. Sorry boys and girls, but sing along with me, "Australians all let us rejoice, for we are young and free, something something…".

The Jacarandas

The Jacarandas are raining! And they've all decided to do it at the same time. Just today they've all let their purple flowers drop fluttering to the ground, creating a carpet to soften the bitumen roads and concrete paths. They always look amazing in bloom, heralding the start of the warmer weather with their big colourful statement. But I've never seen them disrobe all at once like this before. Perhaps it's the combination of a strongish breeze and how it's suddenly gotten warm again after a cold snap. Who cares why? The jacarandas are raining, are snowing, are hailing purple! Summer is almost here.

The alarming thing

The alarming thing about earth tremors is the feeling of helplessness. Our senses of certainty and security are shaken to the earth's core. There are things we take for granted – the sky above, the earth below. A tremor tells us to not even trust these. So besides the fear of things falling on top of us, it's a very emotional terror.

I have experienced many tremors. If you live in Wellington, New Zealand you experience them every day, until it gets to the point when you don't even look-up from your desk. But these are little things, despite the evidence of the once great quake that scars a hill right in the city centre. You can clearly see exactly where the earth separated itself that time.

There was a particularly bad one in Bali when we were staying in a very closed-in resort, made-up of narrow alleyways hedged on both sides with twelve-foot walls. We knew that if things started to crumble we'd be locked about a hundred yards in.

But my very worst was twenty floors up in a skyscraper that had a metal frame. It overlooked Sydney Harbour, and during the tremor the whole building swayed, the horizon dipping to the left and then the right. If it went we were gone.

If a skyscraper can be made to dance, if the earth can make us lose our footing, how certain is anything? Imagine if a day comes and the sun doesn't rise.

I don't know

I don't know if plants have feelings, but just in case I make sure to quickly remove any dead leaves that have fallen from our pot plants. How would you like it if you were alive and vital and bursting with green, only to have to look down at the browning carcasses of your dead fellows?

When we set the table

When we set the table for dinners with friends, it can be like a display of our wedding gifts. The crisp white cotton table clothe, matching napkins, a beautiful white china bowl with silver trim, a quirky Scandinavian-designed water jug that acts like a thermosflask. It is a happy thing to do and share, especially if any of the gift givers are there. They always joke that we only brought their gift out for them, and it will get quickly disappeared as soon as they leave - into a box with a label bearing their name. But it's not true, and because it all matches so well, everyone knows it's not. It's still good to have the joke though.

Things that can be broken

Bones
Hearts
Glass
China
Furniture
Memories
Wills
Lights
Thoughts
Waves
Devotions
Desires
Clouds
Buildings
Doors
Bottles
Promises

Sportspeople talk

Sportspeople talk about being 'In The Zone'. And I have experienced this while running. It's like you've lost your peripheral vision and there's only what's immediately in front of you, and your body stops knowing what it's doing. It's running on automatic, without a pain or a strain or care of any sort. Your legs are just going out in front of you, and you look down on them as if they're not even your own. You're going as fast as you're ever going to go, yet it's totally effortless.

But this is nothing compared to The Zone of Mania. It can go for days. Take all of the above and multiply it by a thousand and then you have not begun to describe it. You can, and do, do anything and everything. And it's all fun, until someone gets hurt.

Looking back

Looking back I can see why some people I wanted to be close to didn't want to be close to me. It's the Icarus affect. Think of the sun as my craziness and you get the idea. At times I would have this build-up of tremendous power in the centre of my chest, not a heart-bursting glow, but more a hard nucleus ripe for atomic fusion. I still get that feeling when I'm getting manic. It's then that my mind must play Daedalus.

My sculpture

My sculpture can be a little off-putting, yet strangely appealing at the same time. It is all of a theme, always using jars. I take the jars and stick things in them or on them or both. I use jars because they are containers. It says something about the things we keep inside. I often combine them with dolls. I pull the dolls apart and put the head on the top of the lid, split the body in two and place it front and back, then have the separated arms and legs sticking out. I paint them all silver, except in places where I want what is inside to be seen. The silver represents the future, like bad sci-fi. There's a baby-doll jar with a plastic rat inside. Another baby-doll one with a coin wedged in the doll's mouth and another stuck out its bottom, above a collection of chocolate gold coins. I call that one 'Grandiosity'. Sometimes I cut toys in half and make it look like they're passing through the jar – a jet fighter, farm animals, cars. Other ones have the mess of life stuck all over them - like the contents of the drawer we have filled with bits and pieces emptied onto them.

It's good to have a creative outlet. Especially in a culture that has separated out all the different talents to specializations owned by few and off-putting to the amateur. The aborigines show us how it could be done. They all paint, all dance, all sing, all make music, all act-out their shared stories. The one thing that tells us just how much damage we have done them, is the fact that now aboriginal painting is sold like Western art, according to the signature.

My first attempt at therapy

My first attempt at therapy was years before the bi-polar diagnosis and after a plane incident. I had just spent a week at a health retreat recovering from a punishing work schedule, during which I was doing some highly secret work for an airline. There was a proposed merger and it was a sensitive national issue. The week away had done me the world of good, and I boarded the plane looking forward to getting home.

Ten minutes out it felt like the plane had hit a mountain – the lights went out, the plane dropped so fast the sky outside the windows went from rich blue to a light blue. I was sitting above the wing and looked out to see the engine ripping itself apart and in flames. Everyone saw it and that created panic. People threw-up. One of the flight attendants ran down an aisle in tears. It was not reassuring. The captain came on and said we would be returning to the airport. It took about twenty minutes to fly in circles and drop the fuel. When it came time to land we were told to go into the Advance Brace position; hands over our heads and heads between our knees. The plane dropped hard onto the tarmac. Apparently the wing holding the engine had been damaged and the pilot was unable to use the flaps to affect the landing. He had to just drop and pull-on the brake. They then kept us in the plane for another half hour. Later I was to discover that this was because they were afraid the heat from the overworked brakes might cause an explosion, so we were safer inside than out. After almost a full day spent in the terminal they got us a new plane and we were off again. I was unconcerned, getting on the new plane without a tremor.

The problem was the next day. I went to my gym and got onto one of those weight machines where you have to buckle yourself in. As I went to do this my hands started to tremble, I couldn't get the buckle together, I began sobbing uncontrollably. The day after it happened again, this time on a short flight for business. I wasn't even thinking about being on a plane, and again it was only when I went to secure the buckle that the same problems occurred. But my colleagues got me through it and we did our

Anthony Peck

business at the other end. But it happened yet again on the way home. That's when I booked in to see a therapist.

He was a really nice guy who welcomed me into his office and let me tell him about what was happening. He got me to do an exercise that brought up a lot of old anger, nothing to do with the incident. It got quite physical, and he was visibly scared as a chair flew across his desk and bounced off the wall behind. Once I'd settled he assured me that the flight failure had set-off some deep-seated emotions, and if I liked I could come back regularly and sort it all out. He said I wouldn't have trouble on a plane again. And he was right, I never have. But I didn't go back to him. I was too frightened. I'd avoided all those emotions the first time around, I didn't want to have to finally deal with them.

The proposed merger never happened. And the irony was that I was flying on one of the planes owned by one side of the proposed merger, and it had been the maintenance crew from the airline on the other side that had failed to catch the fault that led to the engine blow-up. Mind you, I had neglected the opportunity to do my own maintenance, and that ended-up with its own sort of implosion.

My fingernails itch

My fingernails itch from time to time. Nothing extreme, just enough to annoy, and then not enough to complain about. It's every day, so I'm used to it. It's not the nails themselves of course, just the skin around their edges. I spread my fingers and push the tips down on my thigh and sought of pump them. It doesn't make it go away, but gives a moment's relief. I think it's the drugs, as I feel it most at night after I've taken them. Little reminders can sometimes be the most powerful.

Sometimes I'm not

Sometimes I'm not as good as I may seem, especially during a high. But there's a fragility there. Without vigilance I know I could break. Routine has become important to me. No surprises. Small things can set me to wobbling, while the big crashes I'm always looking out for. It's early in my treatment yet. I have to keep reminding myself of that. Not too much should be expected. I look forward to the day when my control is absolute, if that is ever poissible. Till then I walk the ledge, arms stretched out, mind focused. Having fallen once I dare never fall again.

A cleansing bath

A cleansing bath can take the edge off pain. In a powerful depression my body aches as if I've run a marathon, or paddled my board beyond sight of land. I take myself to bed, but usually don't sleep, just lay there and nurse the pain. I pull a pillow to me and squeeze it tight and hold on. I'm waiting for this pain to pass and free me to my normal self again. If feeling great scores ten, then I am one or two or zero. My head hangs, I avoid eyes and say only the necessary. There's guilt attached too – for letting Camille down, for failing myself, for failing at life. I know it cannot last forever. But right now is my forever, and the ache goes right through. I am canceling plans and avoiding effort. This is no crying sickness, more like taking a beating, when the initial dull bone-crunching remains. I can barely lift my arms, even to defend myself. I sit in the bath and throw handfuls of water over my head, trying for the cleansing pictured along the Ganges. And here I find myself unable to stick with one description or metaphor, struggling with all I have of language to name what simply cannot be washed away.

It's a privilege

It's a privilege to live in a green city. As you come in to land, Sydney looks all green, interrupted only by the blue slither of the harbour. The red roofs are certainly visible, often coupled with a patch of blue swimming pool, and the bigger roads leave a mark. But for the most part it's the green you notice. Every footpath is dotted with trees, and they often hang over buildings and roads to give a blanketing effect. Approaching Sydney by road the concrete and glass city skyline suddenly appears, but all before you is leafy, until you really get in the thick of it.

The weather is kind too. There is barely a day when it isn't a pleasure to walk somewhere outdoors, a park or café, and enjoy and relax in an atmosphere that is genuinely unhurried. We have lived in places that deny this simple outlet. Desert cities and cities of smog and bustle keep you indoors with the air conditioning. There have been times when I have thought how everyone around me would give almost anything for even half a day of the ease a city like Sydney can give you. I have ached for this green and all it invites, and now I'm in it, I remember as often as I can to be thankful.

Last night I dreamed

Last night I dreamed that I had just moved to India. My hair had grown long and Rastafarian. But I wasn't there to be a mountain-posturing guru. The intent was clearly to work in the city, as most of the dream seemed to be taken-up with deciding whether to take a house or live in a hotel. I was imagining the hotel cupboard filled with my clothes and deciding there would be enough space. It would mean I wouldn't have to bring all my furnishings, the way I have always done from country to country. I looked for a barber to cut my hair, but unable to find one I attempted to cut it myself, but that only seemed to make it grow back more. I remember feeling completely unbalanced, unsure, concerned for my prospects, and woke with nothing resolved.

I have often thought that if there is such a thing as past lives, then I was once a monk, training for years in solitude. But in this life my task is to go to the city and practice all I have learned under the test of everyday living. My job is not to preach, but to remain true to the way of Zen. If this is so, then I don't know how I'm doing. Some days are good, some bad, sometimes I forget the things that will keep me balanced. The trick is to keep the vessel of myself empty so that all things can pass in and out, with none of the clinging that can hurt. Perhaps that is the struggle of my dream. Perhaps the best way for a monk to live is in a Novotel.

My physical wounds

My physical wounds are for the most part healed and not worth mentioning. It's my mind that's got a hernia. Heavy loads are too much. Short spurts of thinking are fine, but when I try to lift a weight and hold it there for a time, that's when I feel the damage. And I used to be such a great lifter. It's what I prided myself on. It was part of my identity. My sudden fall from strength has leap-frogged me to an incapacity that should have been a long way into my aged future. Yet here it is, and now I have to look at the size of the box before I attempt to tackle it.

People seem very different

People seem very different to me now. In the early days of my diagnosis I was hungry to meet other people with manic depression and joined a support group. It was great. I got what I was looking for – a level of understanding and consideration that could only come from direct experience. But I got a lot more as well. I saw how different we all were. We came from different backgrounds. Our experiences with manic depression were all different. We were all managing it differently. And each time we met, we were at different points between the manic and the depressive.

In the end I had to give it up. It hurt to turn-up every two weeks and see who was in bad shape this time. Every meeting there was someone you wanted to weep for, to hold, to solve all their problems. Yet the last meeting in which you saw this suffering person, it was they who was the strong one. The whole thing became really disorienting. I guess I wasn't as up to the support bit as I'd hoped.

Today I met two very different people. Or rather, in the past I would have thought of them as very different. But all I could see were similarities - between them and with me. It got me wondering what has changed so fundamentally that I am seeing the unity of people and not the separations. And the difference is my thinking, retrained by experts. I think I've lost some of my symptomatic Grandiosity. When you don't stand above everyone you stand amongst them, rubbing shoulders, and feeling so much better.

I used to think

I used to think that it was because I'm a man that I'm somewhat disconnected from life. I had it all worked out. It was women who owned the earth, as well they should. After all, they're the ones who carry the species forward. Men float unless tied to a woman. Unattached men are lucky not to drift into space altogether, being only held by a loose gravity that keeps them just within the atmosphere, still within sight of humanity. Sometimes it felt that with only a little propulsion I could be lost forever.

I used to think that I was so hot on my bicycle, overtaking people. Until it dawned on me that maybe the people I was overtaking had been riding for a hundred kilometers more than me. I was on fresh legs while they were on their last. That's why I now know comparisons are worthless.

I used to think that I could heal myself in this lifetime from any of the ills that had befallen me and made me less than whole. Now I just try to think that, and hope it will be enough.

When you get older

When you get older you spend more time looking at the surf before going in. As a nipper you don't even look-up, just get that leash on and head out as fast as you can to where everyone else is grouped. You don't know yet that it's important to read the water. It can tell you things that are going to be useful to you once you're out there. It points you in the right direction for the sort of waves you can do most with, knowing your own style. It tells you the easiest way out the back from the shore, and which way to head once you've gotten off a wave. It even tells where to get off the wave, alerting you to the fact that pumping everything out of the wave may not give you much, and your energy is better spent returning back for the next one. You can judge the speed of the wave, which in turn tells you a lot about the best way to ride it. It helps you judge the time between sets, and how many waves you can expect in each one, and which of those you should choose.

As a young surfer I always wondered at how the older guys always seemed to be in the right spot, got smashed less often, rode the best waves. It isn't all about time spent in the water. It's got a lot to do with waiting and watching from the sand.

Grand Finals

Grand Finals don't always put on the best show for the sport. There's too much pressure. The players crowd the ball like school kids do - moving in a congealed mass around what may as well be a sticky toffee. Defence usually wins these encounters, when it's attack that's most watchable. With the whole year on the line, all other comers having been dealt with, the final two teams play for a claim of besting that is usually only marginally true, but in the aftermatch will appear as a chasm. There are no second places in a Grand Final, and on that premise they are spoiled for half the supporters before they've even begun, they just don't know it yet.

As a kid Grand Final Day was awesome. It wasn't like now when there are so many sports to follow. Back then it was just Rugby League, so Grand Final Day was it – everybody watched. I never cared much for the game, so on that "special day that only comes once a year" I would head out onto the empty streets with my scooter. It was eerie how dead it was. And heavenly. I would take off from the tops of the steepest hills I could find, knowing that I could ride straight down the middle totally unmolested and carefree. I had the world to myself and a set of wheels. On Grand Final Day I was the winner.

Frank Sinatra, Dean Martin, Jerry Lewis and Tony Bennett

Frank Sinatra, Dean Martin, Jerry Lewis and Tony Bennett are my American heroes. I have seen three and honoured the fourth.

Frank Sinatra I saw in Sydney during his last Australian tour, at a time when his shows were famously hit and miss. Fortunately he was fantastic on that night. No particular song stands out, but he was every bit as amazing as I had always felt. The warm-up act was Steve Lawrence and Eddie Gorme, which was a last minute surprise, as I'd only gotten the tickets late. I took my mother and father, who loved it, especially as Frank was equally a favourite of my father's. There's not a lot to say about Frank, except he was Frank, and all that history and aura, and the magic of the music and his voice, was right there. A spotlight and a microphone was all he needed. I don't think I blinked even once.

Jerry Lewis was the same. I just never wanted him to end. Here was a man of eighty-three being a naughty nine-year-old boy. He was brave enough to play clips from when he was in his twenties, losing nothing as the lights went up and returned to his elderly frame propped-up by a microphone stand he leant on heavily. For long moments my eyes were fixed on him and I felt no regret for not having seen him earlier. It was all there, he was all there, and we could have been in a theatre in Miami in the fifties, but were in an old converted cinema in Sydney, and that was just fine.

Tony Bennett was smooth, but without the awesome voice I have on albums. His act was honed. So honed that after seeing him in concert I was disappointed to see a TV performance where he repeated the act by the syllable, including the cute side-patter. But hey, he's earned it. I did have the privilege of meeting him once. I was at the famous Spago restaurant in L.A. and in he walked. I couldn't resist but go up to him and introduce myself. "What's you're name?" He asked. "Tony." "Great name."

Dean I never saw, but what an awesome guy. He could sing, play straight-man to Jerry, and believe it or not, probably earned more than Sinatra. I can remember the day he died vividly. I was in Phuket on holiday when I saw it in the evening news. It was a doubly momentous night for me because it was the first day of the cricket Test match that would decide the fate of one of Australia's most lovable batsmen, David Boone. Good old Boonie had had a pretty lean time of it lately, and if he didn't perform in this Test he would mostly likely be dropped.

I took myself off to Phuket's bar district, found a place playing the match, and proceeded to drink heavily while I watched. It made sense to drink doubly heavily with two good causes in my heart – drowning my sorrows for Dean, and supporting Boonie at the same time. Boonie was magnificent. Under the greatest pressure of his career he scored a ton. My heart smiled.

It took some of the sting out of the loss of Dean, though I didn't for a moment forget him. Sweet and Sour, my heart runneth over. And boy did I drink. The cricket finished at about 5am. The bar I was in was the last to bring down its shutter. The place was almost empty. I went to a curbside food vendor and bought half a chicken on a stick, sat in the gutter, and tried to soak up some of the alcohol. That's when a six-foot tall transvestite grabbed me by the arm and tried to drag me away with them. "You come home with me pretty boy. I no charge you. Come free!" I laughed him/her off and he/she laughed too.

I stumbled back to my resort, sozzled but triumphant. I had seen Boonie through and farewelled Dean in style. The transvestite was the icing on the cake. Knowing his act often involved him feigning drunkenness and suggested debauchery, I thought Dean would have been particularly proud.

Celebrity

Celebrity is one of the saddest things I have ever known. As the newly anointed celebrate their supposed attainment, their fate is too easily written into the script. And it's always the same script, so any surprise when things start to go wrong, as they inevitably do, just makes it all the more tragic. Because the surprise also belongs to the audience, implicating them in the farce too. Nobody gains by our modern disease. And now you can do it to yourself on Facebook and Twitter.

The only thing anyone said

The only thing anyone said at school that I remember, was by one of our history teachers. Someone in the class had made a comment about someone else being "up-themselves". The teacher was a short man, maybe only five foot, but he was ferocious, and a Vietnam Vet, which he expressed through his every grisly sinew. "Do you think Alexander the Great didn't have to be up-himself to conquer most of the known world?"

The best thing I remember being said to me while I was in hospital was this little suggestion Jan brought over from Cousin Shane - "You should have worn a cape."

Writing

Writing has always been about truth for me. Not necessarily some great Truth, but the truth in whatever I am writing about. That even includes writing for advertising. If you can find the truth in a product - the thing about it that people will genuinely find useful - then you've got something to sell. People often accuse advertising of lies, and while I am not an apologist for the whole industry, it is worth pointing out the commercial flaw in this accusation.

See companies don't really make money off selling something once, it's repeated sales that advertising is after. If you lie about a product and it doesn't live up to expectations, then people simply won't buy it again. And if they don't buy it the company will go broke, and the agency won't have a product to advertise. So it's in everyone's interest to be a scrupulous as possible with the facts.

This of course does not apply to journalism. The media doesn't have to tell the truth, because you'll switch on the news at six o'clock tomorrow anyway, you'll go online and read your newspaper anyway, you'll buy your regular magazines anyway. What's the worst that can happen? They'll have to write a retraction? Fine, read it in tomorrow's paper.

Truth in any writing has to be single-minded. As soon as another motive is introduced then the truth is compromised. This happens as soon as you start to write as a product. A most obvious example is travel writing. The moment you accept the free hotel room you're faced with an obligation.

Editors have a huge responsibility to the truth. I wouldn't have their job for quids. Easy when they spot some sloppy language, it must get very tricky as soon as they suggest the strengthening of a character, or a variation in plot, or the examination of a preoccupation. When you remove one thing you have to be certain about what will replace it. My own rewrites have often seen the collapsing of the remaining dominoes, a good editor having spotted a gap that just can't be filled.

Truth has a centredness about it. But centredness can be hard to sustain, and may even become dull. Sometimes you have to go around a thing to take readers with you on the way to its core. And truth is often revealed by a lie. You have to take-in the whole work. So even as a reader you can't be lazy with the truth. This larger truth takes emersion in a rhythm, which is often the writer's voice, or the undercurrent of the work - like a subterranean river flowing crookedly to an underground lake of pure truth.

If truth in writing were easy, there'd only have to be one book.

My favourite writers

My favourite writers are so skillful in their craft that it almost causes me a physical pain to read them. This is not envy in any way, more a longing, as if for a departed love. I want to hold their words close to me, have them never end, prove my own affection. If only they could know how much they mean to me, and how unworthy I feel in the presence of their work. The more I ache the greater my admiration for them. Some of my favourite writers are:

Patrick White
Lawrence Durrell
James Joyce
T.S. Eliot
Richard Brautigan
Salman Rushdie
Tim Winton
Ruth Park
Virginia Wolfe
Henry Miller
Ernest Hemingway
Gabriel Garcia Marquez
Italo Calvino
Shakespeare
Wordsworth
Hardy
Martin Amis
Tom Wolfe
Steinbeck

There are other loves whom I read for the content, but these are the ones I read purely for the writing.

A friend of mine

A friend of mine died two days ago in Vietnam where he was working – pneumonia and swine flu. All I can think about is his cold body lying in a foreign morgue. His face is blue.

On the day he died I was thinking about how I hadn't heard from him, though he said he'd call me as soon as he got home, which should have been a few weeks ago, about the time he checked himself into hospital.

I dreamed about his funeral all last night. I can't seem to think past it, like I'm in a room surrounded by walls, each one with an image of him on it. Mostly I'm just sad for him and his family and other friends. And a small part thinks that could have been me. But that's the limit of it before my mind comes up hard against his blue face again. As if that's what death is – a thought beyond which there are no other thoughts.

My grandfather's old radio

My grandfather's old radio runs on valves. You turn it on and wait for the green bulb to gradually brighten, matched by the steadily increasing volume as it comes to life. It's quite big for a radio – one foot high and about two feet wide – and cased in baker light. He'd fallen in love with it the day he saw it in a Port Moresby store, when he and Grandma visited us there in the early sixties. I was given it after Grandma died, which was about ten years after grandfather.

Before it was given to me it had spent its life in the faux fireplace next to grandfather's sacred reclining chair. He would always be at the short wave controls, listening in to radio from as far away as Russia. Or he'd have the rugby league on, playing at full blast. He was a fabulous man, employed as a fitter and turner down at the wharfs, and was a strong union member and socialist. His bookshelves only seemed to have socialist authors, like the Australian Frank Hardy. It was him and his colleagues who went on strike for five months to win worker's rights such as the forty-hour week. I don't know how he'd cope if he saw his grandchildren regularly putting in over fifty.

But the radio still works, and I've even managed to find more valves in case the old ones break. Whenever I look at it I get the feeling of his gentleness, often slow to come to life, but enduring and bright to the end.

Anthony Peck

The flies are back

The flies are back in our living room, which means summer's on its way. There's either three or five of them circling the middle of the room, in a crazy pattern only they know the rules of. They're always in the same spot, directly below the chandelier. We don't dislike them or make any effort to kill them. They're a feature. And they're not doing anyone harm. I sometimes watch them for minutes at a time. The other day I wondered out loud if they were the same ones from last summer, but Camille assured me they were the next generation. And yet they do exactly the same things. It might be interesting to record their family tree.

You don't hear people

You don't hear people tell a lot of jokes these days. It's more likely they'll describe a video they saw on YouTube, or recount a funny email they've received. It's the theatre of telling jokes that I miss. The way you have to do the funny accents and build the story. You have to put yourself out there and risk getting razzed if you fall flat. But the new world is not like that. There are props for everything. PowerPoint presentations you can download to prove any point. 'Books for Dummies' on every topic. In fact, if people were still telling jokes, I'm sure someone would invent Joke Insurance, just in case.

Annoying things

Waking too early
Having the last mouthful taken from your plate
Wanting something and finding you've just run out
Rain or bad light stopping the cricket
Finding you've only recorded half the show you wanted to watch
Pages missing from a book

It seems they're all about interruptions to things you would normally enjoy to the end. So this list could be titled 'Interruptions' instead. But first and foremost they are all truly annoying.

It was years ago

It was years ago on my first trip overseas, when the world was not nearly so homogenous. These days you get off a plane and you could be just about anywhere. There'll be a McDonalds and a GAP, and everyone will be wearing the same clothes that you can get in Brisbane or Budapest. But back then globalization hadn't hit, and everywhere you went opened-up a whole new world to discover.

I'd already spent a month in Paris, then Rome, Florence, Venice – all by train. I'd pretty much run out of money in Venice and figured the only way to stretch my money was to go somewhere really cheap. So using my one month Europass train ticket, I headed to Salerno, a seaside village in the south of Italy.

After god knows how many hours on the train I finally arrived. I don't know how I picked it in the first place, but there I was. I found the cheapest pensionné, which was empty, it being the middle of winter and low season.

Then, having settled into my room, I went out to explore the place. At first there was no one about, but I kept walking until the streets opened up to a square, right by the water's edge. There was a crowd of people and I wondered what the event was? So I waded in. The crowd was thin at the edges, gradually getting more intense as I closed in on what I thought might be some sort of performance at the centre. But before I knew it the crowd was thinning out again. There had been nothing at the centre at all, it was simply the people of the town coming out for their weekend promenade.

This was better than a show. Realising what was happening, I stood back and watched with fascination. Everyone knew each other. It was a constant series of greetings and farewells – arms were thrown in the air, cheeks were kissed, shoulders squeezed. All ages were represented. Children ran in zig-zags between adult bodies in a well rehearsed game. This was all very new to me and seemed a good way to be. I had grown-up barely knowing the people who lived next door, let alone throughout the neighbourhood. These southern Italians proved you don't need an event to bring people together, you just need people. I wonder if they're still doing it today?

Festivals

Festivals are defined by the need for everyone to participate. In days of yore the whole village would turn out to celebrate the harvest, or the longest day, or the shortest day, or whatever. Everyone would go to weddings or funerals. Youths would be inducted into adulthood. The times of year and the milestones of life were a communal affair. Now a festival is a paid event, usually involving bands and corporate sponsorship.

Whatever I am reading

Whatever I am reading affects the way I think. It also affects the way I write, but this you can get under control. It's the hold it has over my mind that can either elevate me or bring me down. I put it down to being perhaps too empathetic. Like watching an old episode of Batman. I get really worried about whether or not the Dynamic Duo will free themselves from the chains they have holding them over a boiling vat of oil. And I mean really worried. I can barely watch, and yet am glued to the set like a five-year-old.

With reading there's the extra engagement of being the one in charge of the words, so to speak. It's up to me to read them. I could just close the pages and put the book away. But even then the cadence of the words becomes the rhythm of my own thoughts. The vocabulary becomes mine.

So I've learned to be selective. On holidays I read trash, like old M*A*S*H paperbacks, or the very easy Rumpole of the Bailey. How can you loosen-up when Salmun Rushdie is in the middle of an exposition on Partition, seen through the eyes of a child?

Lawrence Durrell's 'The Avignon Quintet'

Lawrence Durrell's 'The Avignon Quintet' is a beast of a book. I have read no critiques, spoken with no one on the subject, and have only my own theory. But I do have a theory. You see Durrell significantly outlived his literary age. Having written under the tutelage of Anaïs Nin and Henry Miller, he was of that time, including Joyce and Hemingway and Faulkner and Woolfe and all that tribe. But having outstayed the lot of them, he was able to take what they were doing with the novel and propel it to its ultimate expression, in a book that is the last of those sort of books, and perhaps even the death of the novel altogether.

Because what he achieved with 'Avignon' is a book you can never stop reading. A book that is vast in length, boundless in the range of topics it examines, and so complicated in terms of character and plot, that by the time you get to the end you naturally turn back to the beginning and start again. Having forgotten the start there is no finish. You have to keep going and restarting and going and it never ceases pushing you forward. There are books piling-up beside my bed that I want to read but may never get to. And in a funny way I'm not really disappointed, because I'm sure that whatever lies between their covers is somewhere within 'Avignon'. It's all going to be there, I just have to keep going in and finding it. Sweet sweet agony.

As I write this I remember the occasion when I met Mr. Durrell. It was at the famous Olde Shakespeare Bookshop on the left bank of Paris, just across from Notre Dame. After a quick check of publication dates I realize it must have been the launch of 'Quinx', the last of the 'Quintet'. It was a pretty busy night and I had gotten there late, so missed all the official bits. I didn't know anything about Durrell then, except that he was important and knew Henry Miller, who was a big hero of mine at that time. I did get to shake his hand though. To think it has taken me all these years to get to the book. A good thing too, because I don't think I could have coped with it then.

As it was I was recovering from a vicious hangover earned the night before. A street away from the bookshop I had spent the previous night in the company of a punk rock band and their entourage. I had met the entourage while getting a sandwich greche from a street vendor at lunch. We got to talking, and they invited me to see the band that night. They were a pretty rough bunch, drinking wine straight from gallon bottles, which they handed around unceremoniously. They were already drunk when we met, and they announced that that night they would be celebrating the fiftieth consecutive attendance at the band's gigs by one of their number. They had been touring with the band all through Europe and would be going home to England after this last show. So passions were running high.

That night I had gotten drunk with them. The niteclub was tiny and cavernous, the band atrocious, and the fans were just short of violent. I was quite tiny then, about 50kg, and when it came to the slam dancing, they'd just pick me up and throw me from one end of the club to the other. I'd gotten drunk enough not to feel the bruising, and laughed as I flew. When it was all over I stumbled into the Paris winter night drenched in sweat, which froze on my body by the time I got to my cheap little hotel. I recall seeing the little flyer about the Lawrence Durrell event pasted on the wall of the spiral staircase, and reminding myself that I shouldn't forget to go. It was a long climb up those stairs, my mind fixed on forcing myself to remember the Durrell event. Up and up I went, round and round. It seems it has always been this way for Lawrence Durrell and me.

For what it's worth

For what it's worth we have crystals in the apartment. I've attempted to select and set them out according to the rules of Feng Shui. I'm not at all sure I've got it right. They're meant to be in a configuration that will make us wealthy. In one corner is a pure white crystal ball, around eight kilograms, on a bed of crushed green crystals speckled with ovals of fine green jade, and surrounded by sticks of nine different crystals - ranging in colours from black with a gold vein, to pinks, amber, green and grey. In the opposite corner is a plant, designed to invite the energy of life, which is somehow meant to be magnified through the white crystal opposite. The alternative is to have one of those big purple crystals that are formed in their own little cave-like frame, but our one of those stands facing the door. Behind the crystals and the plant are crystal glasses with water and Himalayan salt in them, purifying any energy that passes through them.

Like I say, I'm not sure if any of this is right, but it was the best advice I got one day from a Chinese taxi driver. We don't seem to be getting any richer, but that doesn't stop us from feeling that way. We've only got to look at the crystals to see something beautiful.

Today we looked

Today we looked at two-week-old puppies, one of which will be ours in another six weeks. It felt good to get out of the city and be surrounded by just trees. I like that section of the highway as well, the way it cuts through sandstone hills. It's easy to imagine the hard work that was done years ago to make these cuttings. They've been formed so neatly, as if by artisans of old, but really using a lot of dynamite and the hard labour of road workers with basic skills. But they did it and did it well. And we zoomed through the landscape they'd cleared to a litter of eight, not yet with their sight or hearing, all bundled together to give each other comfort and reassurance.

The puppies only just filled your hand. The breeder was far more robust with them than we dared to be, but I'm sure that will come to us. They were too small for us to pick exactly which one would be ours, but the breeder assured us that on our next visit she'd be able to indicate more of their individual personalities.

We didn't talk much on the way home. Perhaps we'd seen enough of life to not have to say anything. I barely even noticed the sandstone cuttings, or the trees, off in my own little puppy heaven.

When my dreams

When my dreams get too graphic that's when I know there's something I'm holding in. I have always suffered from my dreams. When I was three they would find me trying to climb the wall at the head of my bed, attempting to get away from the chasing tigers. My first overseas trip was curtailed by dreams so dramatic that I feared going to sleep. I would see members of my family in pools of blood. So it became imperative to get home and check on them. Still I wake in terror, or Camille wakes me to get me out of some imaginary pickle I've gotten myself into. Last night an evil woman forced me into a tent and stuck some sort of primitive sedation stick into my neck, and then with another woman proceeded to eat me alive. I think they'd gotten to my elbows by the time my choking sounds woke Camille, who then woke me.

Sleep is the most precious commodity of all to someone with bi-polar. You know there's something going wrong when you stop having enough. It's the clearest sign of all, and one of the worst symptoms. Even with reasonably heavy medication you can wake bug-eyed after just a few hours. If you get three nights in a row like this it's time to consult your doctor. You can get it going up or down. I've gotten into the habit of protecting my sleep - not accepting invitations that will see me having to stay up late, taping shows I like but that run past my bedtime. We also need more sleep than everyone else. Ten to twelve hours seems about right.

If you know someone with bi-polar this thing with the sleep is the most important thing you should know about them and that you can help them with. We prefer lunches to dinners, matinees to evening shows. Traveling across time zones is something we need to manage carefully. And if we say we're tired, we often mean so much more.

I once convinced

I once convinced a colleague that the answer to every question was my name. It was a time when I was quite mad. Job's gone over budget? "Say 'Tony Peck'." One of the staff is dropping the ball. "Say 'Tony Peck'." Client looks like they're about to walk. "Say 'Tony Peck'."

I was very depressed at the time and seemed to need to assert my identity. At the same time it illustrated one of my triggers. By putting everyone else's needs before my own I could get myself into a state where the only way I could cope was to overcompensate and be the total answer to any problem. I was dragging myself down and down.

Depression isn't just about moping around. For me it is quite an agitated state. Rather than being subdued, I can be manic in my depression. It isn't just my identity I'm struggling to hold onto, it's my life.

The length of a poem

The length of a poem
is as far as
I will let
a tear
fall

The length of a poem
is as long as
I will let
a tear
last

I have always felt most comfortable

I have always felt most comfortable in front of a crowd. The bigger the crowd, the better I feel. A presentation to one or two people is hard to get revved-up about. You don't want to blast them out of the room. To a dozen or more there's more room to walk about and get a bit theatrical. Give them turns in receiving your full attention. Fifty starts to feel about right. Now there are no fears of interruptions. People hold their comments until you invite them, because they know that if they start then everyone could start. At fifty it's your room and you can walk from side to side, down the centre aisle, wherever you want. You are almost anonymous now. You're the presenter and they are the audience.

At school I got my practice on a thousand. All boys, and none of them were particularly willing me on. To gather the whole school required using the biggest playground, at the centre of which a brick stage had been constructed. It was there we gathered for Mass on special occasions. They got me to do the Readings. I'd also get to say a few words to visiting dignitaries. School plays were my biggest test though, especially as I usually had the female role. Well, in an all-boy school someone had to do it. We did have a relationship of sorts with a girls' school a secure few railway stations away, but there was no way any girl was going to be considered safe spending her after-school hours rehearsing in our grounds.

We were a pretty rough bunch. Inner city, working class, crammed into a concrete and brick jungle with not a blade of grass. Class sizes were all at least fifty, and the playgrounds were tiny enough to create their own frustrations. In Year Six over two hundred boys were expected to share a tennis court. The school's theme was to not produce scholars, but good people. A good motivation, but restrictive in it's vision. The best we were expected to be was public servants or police, and at the very pinnacle - teachers.

It was considered enough just to keep us in check, which wasn't always successful. There were police escorts for the school buses at times. Then there was the big brawl planned in our final year with a neighbouring school, where every boy carried a weapon in his bag. Squad cars circled the block that day and shepherded us back through the gates. There was a lot more of this sort of stuff, but looking back it wasn't that frightening. Like prison, I guess you get used to the unspoken laws.

And I wore dresses. Playing Calpurnia in Julius Caesar I brought down the house. The lights were meant to go down at the end of one scene while I remained alone on stage reclining on a chaisse lounge. But the lighting guy had missed his cue. The first time I spoke the front few rows heard and giggled. "Turn down the lights…" I threw over my shoulder. The next time my voice was louder and carried further, "Turn down the lights…". Still nothing. So now I bellowed in as gruff a voice as I could manage, "Would you turn off the bloody lights!" Lights out, big laughs. I may have been wearing a dress but I knew how to handle this crowd. Who would have guessed they'd been training me for a lifetime of presenting?

The other day my psychologist picked-up on my ability to present, even in therapy. It seems I talk about feeling vulnerable, but not for long, switching instead to talking-up the positives. We discussed how I have trained people in my life to think I'm always o.k., I'll always sort things out. Now, even when I'm at my most vulnerable, all they see is the progress and not the sometimes difficulty. And it's all my own fault – I've taught them not to nurture me. But that's o.k., I'm learning to nurture myself.

I have a picture of myself at the age of ten, which I look at from time to time, reassuring the young me that he's going to be looked after, and that everything will be alright. So you see, I'm still doing it. "Would you turn on the bloody lights!?"

I purchased

I purchased our lounge in Bahrain during an up time. It's the only excuse I can offer. There's a three-seater, a two-seater and a single-seater. They're red, with a damask floral pattern. The piping is gold and red striped. The arms are generously rounded. The backings have a thick top edge of red velvet and raise majestically to a regal summit. The height of this summit varies according to the size of the individual sofas. The three-seater sits so high we were unable to get it through the door of the apartment, so it lives in storage. Each sofa has red velvet back cushions edged with tassels. Tassels also run around the bottom edges of each sofa and around all the edges of the sitting cushions. There are a lot of tassels. And the overall impression is of an exotic grandeur you might expect in a Persian court, or a tasteless wax museum.

Newcomers to the house always appear assaulted by them on first viewing, but after a short while find themselves very cosy. Those who take the single-seater, their arms spread wider than usual across its breadth, and resting in Sphinx-like calm, are prone to put on airs. It is like taking to a throne after all. And the impression is in no way lessened when their feet rest upon the ottoman, which is like a red and golden orb; again, heavily tasseled.

The TV cabinet was bought on the same day – dark wood, ornate copper handles, lots of wooden curves and detailing. Cousin Shane ventured the overall impression as "pretentious". If only it were that simple. And you can't deny the comfort.

Anthony Peck

Persian carpets

Persian carpets are something I never thought I'd fall for, but I have. They're like great art, only on the floor. I know some people put them on the walls, especially the more valuable and fragile ones, but that somehow seems wrong to me. Though it's not a particularly strong feeling, just a preference.

I have only shopped for rugs twice. Once in Bahrain when we bought nine new rugs in the space of under an hour before leaving the country, with me hobbling on my broken feet through the markets. Cheap, but all very nice, and they look good now spread through the apartment.

The other spree was in Jeddah, when I got six rugs in a moment of some mania. I was there with a colleague for the weekend and figured it could be profitable to get antique rugs at Saudi prices, which I was told would be cheaper than elsewhere. Apparently a lot of pilgrims use their rugs as currency when they go to Saudi for their trip to Mecca. At the end of Ramadan traders stand at the doors of the airport and hand over cash for rugs, which the pilgrims use to pay for their trip. I'd read that Afghan Street was the place to go, so we headed off from the hotel in search of our treasures.

Looking back I was on a high already. My colleague was alarmed when I stopped the first car coming along the road and asked for a lift. "Are you sure you want to do this?" he asked, as I pushed him into the back seat in front of me. Turns out the driver was a nice young guy from Yemen. We negotiated a price, and he took us to the old souk.

We had lots of fun there, looking at the honeycomb, buying the national costume, and taking photos of the fantastic architecture. I joined a water boy and, to the amusement of the locals, helped him sell some water. We kept asking where Afghan Street was and got pointed every which way. Finally we got directions from someone who seemed to know what they were talking about. So we headed away from the souk, through a light industrial area,

170

until we found ourselves in streets with just houses. We were lost and in the built-up backstreets of Jeddah, where people eyed us suspiciously from doorways, and two little boys playing soccer ran away the moment they saw us.

There were some young guys doing renovations nearby though, and we went and asked them if they knew where Afghan Street was. They didn't speak English, but one of them called someone on their mobile and in less than a minute a big man was standing before us asking what we wanted. He immediately told us he would take us. We got in his car and chatted as he drove. He showed us how he had two fingers missing, putting it down to an accident on the wharfs. But we knew it would be punishment for stealing. He dropped us off, giving us his card, "If you're ever in Jeddah again…".

Afghan Street was a wonder. Everyone was Afghani, as we could tell from their clothes – colour rather than plain white, and with the flat pancake hat. The street had bakeries all along it, and at one we were even allowed to throw the dough onto the ceiling of the kiln. You have never tasted bread like it. There were also a lot of stores selling bed linens. We both bought outlandish gold sets with lots of beading. And finally we found our carpet shop. There were two side-by-side, but we only ever managed to see the one. It was wall-to-wall carpets, with a separate room out the back with various bric-a-brac and furnishings.

We both loved everything in this Aladdin's cave. Our passion was too obvious though, and the father and son owners soon closed the doors to focus on us two prime suckers. I bought six rugs, my friend bought two. They were all from Turkmenistan, pure silk, hand-woven, and over seventy-five years old. We both knew enough to recognize this was so, or close enough. They hadn't bargained on us both having lived in Asia and knowing our way around a price, and I knew we'd done reasonably well when they started to look gloomy.

It was while they were folding the carpets for us that I saw it. It was in the back room, the largest piece of furniture they had. A hundred year old make-up cabinet with mirror, over two metres high and more than a metre and a half wide. Pure rosewood and weighing a ton. It was from Afghanistan, gotten out before the Taliban rode in. Carved with serpents and flowers, and not sticking to the rigid geometric patterning preferred by Islam. I was in a fever from the carpet buying and had to have it. We agreed on a price and I also paid for it to be shipped to my home in Bahrain. For good measure I got them to throw in a walking stick covered in Lapis Lazuli, before leaving the shop five thousand dollars poorer.

The make-up cabinet stands at the end of our bed in Sydney now. The rugs are rolled-up and put away, too precious for a floor with a puppy, and with not enough space on the walls. The walking stick is with my others and some umbrellas in a tall Chinese vase by the front door. As souvenirs they evoke memories, but not necessarily great or shameless ones. Meanwhile the cheap rugs, all factory made, are soft underfoot, easy to maintain, and it doesn't matter if we spill anything on them. They look good too.

Friends far away

Friends far away are my loneliest thing. By far the majority of my friends live elsewhere. We stay in contact by the occasional email, and these are always fraught with wanting to write everything but not wanting to seem desperate or boorish. The phone is somehow inadequate. So much of friendship consists in not having to say anything.

There is 'Down-hill Tiger'

There is 'Down-hill Tiger' and 'Up-hill Tiger' in Chinese painting. 'Down-hill Tiger' is literally prowling down a hillside, whiskers erect, snarling in preparation for its kill, claws sharp and ready. It is a symbol of all that is ravenous and anticipatory in man. There are millions of copies of this painting throughout China. People even refer to someone as a 'Down-hill Tiger' when they are obviously on the hunt for riches, lust, power. 'Up-hill Tiger' is the same beast in a completely different attitude. Having had their fill they are slowly, leisurely, passionlessly making their way back up the hill in languid steps. This is a cat you could pat, so limp it seems. You will often see the two paintings together, one on either side of a doorway.

We have a beautiful version of 'Down-hill Tiger' just outside our bedroom door. It's at least the best I have ever seen. When you look at the tiger's coat you could swear it is moving, so fine is the detailed brushwork. We don't have our 'Up-hill Tiger' yet. The trick is to discover one of equal quality to our 'Down-hill' version. Or have it hunt us down.

This week

This week has been swallows week. Twice I have had the pleasure of their company. I have always loved swallows. The smoothness of their gliding punctuated with short bursts of speed and acrobatic cornering. And they're so little. The other day I was walking through a park and they were using me as some sort of obstacle in their frolics. As I walked they would sweep in front of me, coming in from behind at the left and then turning 180 degrees to fly back past me on my right. Perhaps I was doing something to the airflow. I kept walking and they kept appearing and disappearing in the same loop time and time again. Then suddenly they just stopped, and I was immediately sorry to see them go.

The other time I saw a swallow this week was sitting just inside a car park waiting for Camille with some shopping. It was on a nearby sign, just resting there grooming itself. It looked just like a sparrow at first, but then I noticed the little red cravat it wears at the neck and the elegantly pointed black wings. I wondered what it was doing there under cover. It was a windy day, and the swallow was only just inside, so perhaps it was just taking a breather. But the care of its grooming and the fineness of its ensemble, made me wonder if it wasn't perhaps preparing for something less commonplace.

You know

You know something is no longer bothering you when you stop thinking about it. Then the moment comes when it does occur to you again, and you just shrug your shoulders with a "Humph", and then it's gone again. It feels so good to be released from a trouble, like getting out of a prison.

This year has been one long prison break after another. Learning to retrain my mind so I can control the triggers that used to set me off. Even with a predisposition to manic depression you need never suffer it. It takes trauma to bring it to the surface. Learning to cope means never letting anything become a trauma. You can't help the external ones, but the voices in your head are entirely at your discretion. It takes hard work, but it's the most valuable kind of work. I have learned to replace the negative voices with positive ones. Most importantly, more realistic ones.

My psychologist put it very well the other day. "You've spent your whole life listening to unhelpful voices, why not just swap them with my voice?" So I do the exercises, teaching myself to become my own therapist. "What was the situation? What was the trigger? What were you feeling? What were you thinking? What from your past is similar? What is real about the situation? How have you exaggerated it or made it worse? What is a more realistic way of looking at it? What could you do in the future to handle it better?" All good common sense, and with practice it's meant to become automatic.

Everyone has things ground into them that are unhelpful, that's why I think everyone should have some sort of therapy like this. You've just got to ask yourself, "What am I thinking? WHAT THE HELL WAS I THINKING?"

People are best

People are best in a crisis, and the best people are the best in a crisis. Since my major episode I have been shown generosity beyond what I thought was possible. I have been given the time and support to recover fully. Practicalities aside though, the greatest generosity of all has been how I have been treated with tenderness.

The people looking after my health have shown a kindness that I have never known from medical folk. I think they must ration it and spend the majority on the cases that need it most. Perhaps that is why they are often misunderstood or seen as lacking bedside manner. If you've got a difficult problem they are all over you with care. There's a real encouragement there and recognition that my experience has been hard on me.

My family has been amazing, and I sometimes reflect on just how difficult it must be for them. How do they explain to colleagues or friends what happened to me, without getting embarrassed for themselves or me? How do they keep their composure in my presence, wondering what it's all about or how they may have been implicated. They're not implicated, I was the one who trained them over many years to put up with me the way I was, and to think of me in certain ways. But I imagine there's some soul searching there, though I can only repeat that there needn't be. They don't show me their hurt, and that is their greatest, most generous gift of all. I have seen glimpses and nothing could trouble me more - making their gift all the greater.

Surrender

Surrender is triumphant in moments of passion. You have wondered if she will or won't be yours. Your own desire is certain, but what of hers? Do I make a move? But what if I'm rejected? Summoning all your will, you take her in your arms. Before you even kiss you know the answer. It's in the way her body has surrendered. Then all your doubts evaporate and you are surrendered together. All care, all concern, all weight is gone. And now the thoughts you had of a possible love, become those crazy euphoric feelings of bliss.

With each surrender I have had to make over the past year, I've felt a little better. I have surrendered my negative thoughts, my perfectionism, my false beliefs. Surrender is the best medicine in all things, though hard to permit.

Our wedding

Our wedding was a fantastic day. We kept it simple. I hate weddings that are all about the food. You wait for the food, you eat the food, then wait again for someone to take away the plates. You sit at tables that are big linen-covered barriers to getting to meet people. Speeches are made from the head table, creating a formality that makes you feel like you're at some sort of work conference. Some of the oldies are usually doing sums in their heads to work out how much it all costs, and calculating whether what they spent on their present reflects good value, as if their gift were an entry ticket.

Meanwhile the couple is usually quite young, which means young guests, which means a bunch of guys doing their best to drain the free bar. Then when all the formal stuff is over, it's time to score with one of the bridesmaids. Or with that one single girl at every wedding who seems to get swept away with the romance of it all, and makes herself readily available. It's all a bit awkward, on a day that is meant to be a celebration.

Our wedding was held on the front lawn of Camille's mother's house and in the adjoining park, which runs down to the harbour. We stuck a simple marquee on the lawn, had lots of delicious seafood, meat cuts and salads, and everyone could help themselves. Chairs were dotted around, Persian rugs thrown through the park, and there were plenty of games to keep the kids occupied – badminton, croquet, totem tennis, boulé. We got lucky with the weather, which was sunny and mild. A ferry stop is right by the house and a lot of people arrived that way, so were already in a fun mood, having just had a mini cruise from Circular Quay and under the Sydney Harbour Bridge.

Within half an hour of getting there people were gathered in the park where we had the ceremony, the harbour acting as our backdrop. The ceremony itself was as short as you can make it. Camille and I walked out of the house and across the park to a chorus of gasps as people saw how beautiful Camille and her dress were. And she was beautiful. Strapless, champagne satin with layers of lace. The best thing about it was that it was fun, and she had the pleasure of not having to think about it once all day. She could run around as much as she liked without having to hike-up the bust at any time.

There was no solemnity to the proceedings. People were giggling, taking photos. Camille's mother was held-up with something at the beginning, so I stood there shouting her name before we could begin. Then she and David stood by Camille with her wonderful friends Michelle and Jacqueline, who were the Maid of Honour and Bridesmaid respectively. I had Aunty Jan stand with me. My moment of triumph was when I changed the words "To have and to hold" to "To have and hold onto". Which one of my nieces had a good chuckle at. We exchanged rings, kissed, made small talk with the crowd. The photos took no time. We wanted to celebrate, not have a photo shoot. Overall the photos of the day reflect it well. Lots of candid shots, and even the few posed photos have everyone laughing.

For the rest of the day there were only two brief interruptions to people just wandering about, meeting each other and joining the kids in their games. The first interruption was the speeches. We just stood a few steps up from everyone, who we had gathered together on the front lawn. Camille's mother gave a lovely speech, which gave me too much credit. Then my Uncle Gary stepped-up and made one of his legendary presentations. He talked about what a bum I was, how we had taken twenty years and thousands of miles to work it all out, how we were perfectly suited. For anyone who hadn't heard Gary make a speech before it was unexpectedly high entertainment. For those of us in the know it was absolutely up to standard. For me he was daunting to follow, but fortunately I had a strategy. My good friend Ross had sent an email to read out, which did the job of telling funny tales, painting a picture of me that was suitably ambiguous, and also calmed my nerves. I then thanked everyone, forgetting to thank Camille's Aunty Marge and Uncle Jostein, which I still regret because of how much they contributed. It was during these thanks that I started to choke. It was a bit of a miracle that I was there at all. At that stage my feet were still a bit of a mess and my neck was definitely crooked. All I could do was to end by thanking my family, "Who know how hard it was to get me here..."

The other very slight interruption was for the wedding cake. No speech, we just grabbed a knife and sliced it without bothering to grab absolutely everyone to witness. Then I unexpectedly took Camille in my arms and made a couple of twirls. It would have to do for our wedding dance, but was all either of us wanted. My feet couldn't take more and Camille is shy. So it was just right.

We barely saw each other all day, which apparently is just how it goes for the couple at weddings. It was about ten o'clock when most people had gradually wandered off. In the back garage there was the unlikely scene of David, Uncle Jostein, and Uncle Jim (who was standing wrapped only in a towel), peeling a ton of prawns that had not been eaten and would need to be frozen or else go to waste. All that were left to play with were my brother Matthew and his family. We all sat at table with bench seats on either side as I recounted the following story. Funnily, it was the same story I told in that first hospital in Bahrain, which is one of the few times I remember from then. Jan already knew it, and had egged me on in my sick bed, as we laughed and my ribs ached gratefully with every giggle.

We thought it would be fun

We thought it would be fun, my cousin and I. A guy at my work invited us to join his caving club for a weekend underground in the famous Waitomo caves south of Auckland. My cousin Damien, better known by the suitably laconic tag of The Dood, pictured a wooden boardwalk and a lovely young lady with a torch, leading us on a pleasant tour of the stalagmites and stalactites - switching on light shows from time to time, which would be set-up to bring out the caves' delights, and that would be echoed by appropriate "Ooohs" and "Aaahs" from the appreciative audience. I had the feeling that it might be a little less staged than this - a bit of ducking under low ceilings, no boardwalk, but definitely a frequently trod path. It was neither.

We drove down early and joined the team at their clubhouse. It turned out that most of the club members were part of the local rescue service, so we figured we were in good hands. I made the point of letting them know we were both novices.

The first alarm bell should have rung when our convoy of 4WDs had trouble locating the cave we were to explore. We drove onto farms and talked to their owners about where it could possibly be. I did enquire as to why we were having such difficulty, and was told that no one had been in this particular cave for six years.

When we did eventually find the mouth of the cave it was behind a bush - just a small bush, like the cave opening itself. The team got to work tying a rope to the rear bumper of one of the 4WDs, then dropping it down the hole. So apparently it wasn't a walk-in job. We all got kitted-up, putting on overalls. The others looked at the sneakers The Dood and I were wearing, but no one said anything. We put on helmets with lamps attached to batteries, which we wore on a belt around our waists. Pretty exciting stuff, we thought.
The drop into the cave was about a hundred feet straight vertical into thin air and absolute darkness. When we got to a certain point down the rope one of the people who had gone before us

told us to stop and start swinging. This was necessary to get to the ledge that was our starting point. Below was another hundred feet of clear air before reaching a floor of distant spikes. So getting the swing going with enough impetus to reach the ledge was important. One after the other The Dood and I scrambled onto the ledge, pulled in for the last few feet by one of the burly cavemen. I can't remember whether it was The Dood or I who made this milestone first, but I do remember the look we gave each other when we were reunited. We were both a little shocked.

But there was no time to linger on this thin ledge of just a couple of feet's width. In order for the whole team to get started, those of us who were already down had to quickly get started on the next leg. We were pointed to a hole at the end of the ledge. Not a big hole. Maybe big enough for a medium size dog. We dutifully got down on our stomachs and crawled through for about twenty very tight feet.

It was with relief that we reached a space big enough to sit comfortably and catch our breathe. There were five of our full team of about fifteen huddled there, and we couldn't have fitted more because of the wide gap that opened up on the path ahead. There was another opening off to one side, but we were told that the way through was forward. The gap was about five metres long and a metre or so wide. When we looked down from the edge it was clearly a very long way down. I asked how we were possibly going to get across, expecting ropes and specially designed Batman-style hooks to appear. One of our companions then made a surprising demonstration. He wedged himself across the gap, feet pushing against one wall, his back against the other, the only thing holding him up being the pressure created by his bent body. It was clear that any relaxing of this posture would result in a fatal drop. Moving one foot first, then his back, then the next foot, and so on, he made it across, maintaining the tension through his body all the way. The technique was not easy or natural. When The Dood and I followed we were both studies in concentration. On the other side we were both white, sweating and shaking, having stared death in the face and barely survived the occasional slip.

Four of us made it over before a head appeared through the initial hole and told us we had gone the wrong way, we would have to come back and go through the other opening. This was some relief, as the way we were going we would have to face another gap like the first, albeit shorter. What was upsetting though, was that we had to go back over the initial gap the way we had come, the very terror of which had already weakened us.

The Dood was angry now, and so was I. When we had gotten over the gap I took one of the cavemen aside and told him we'd had enough. "We told you we were novices. We'll just go back to the ledge and someone can haul us up the rope." "Sorry, can't do. You'll be right, there's no more like this."

We went through the other opening and entered a space we could all stand up in. We calmed. The rock floor was wet but not slippery, and there was a beautiful looking wall of stalagmites hanging in the light of our helmet lamps. Unfortunately, the way through meant sliding down the sloping floor on our backs and somehow squeezing below this otherwise inviting wall. The gap between mites and floor was not great and left rips in our overalls, but not enough to be a concern. The cuts were likewise shallow and barely worth mentioning.

On the other side of the stalagmite wall the airiness of the space continued. There was plenty of room to walk, no bending required, though on some occasions we did have to crawl through tight spaces. This seemed to go on for some time. But time was fuzzy down there. We just kept moving forward. And before we knew it we were standing on a reasonably wide ledge looking down into a cavern the size of a tennis court, with a high sweeping ceiling.

It was about thirty feet from the ledge to the floor of the cavern. In the middle of the ledge ahead was a huge boulder, blocking the way for a width of about twelve feet. Now they brought out a rope, securing it with a peg struck into one side of the boulder, which was then crept around spread-eagled by one of the cavemen, inching little by little until he reached the other side and secured the other end of the rope. I wasn't sure how this was going to work, but soon enough it became clear. Everyone was going to perform the spread-eagle maneuver. The rope was there as a 'safety'. It didn't feel that way when I crept my way around, reaching for each hold with desperation. It was actually quite loose, useless in fact, and would do nothing at all to stop a slip that could see me with a busted head sprawled on the stony ground below. It never occurred to me then that all this would be funny one day.

But we got through to the other side of the ledge and managed to have a breather as we passed unhindered to the floor of the cave and across to a tall thin vertical opening, on the other side of which we could hear gurgling water.

Beyond the narrow opening it remained narrow. The walls squeezed us, not quite shoulder width. And they were jagged and sharp. We had come upon an underground stream, about thigh high. As we walked along the walls tore at us, the water was icy, we had to concentrate not to stumble and get our batteries wet. It seemed to go on forever. We later calculated there was about an hour and a half of this. Soaked to the skin, freezing cold, bleeding from our barely protected shoulders.

Finally we reached a place where the water disappeared into a wall of rock and there was a small dry shore hemmed in by more rock, at the bottom of which was a hole. This was not a big hole. A rabbit would have baulked at it. We were assured it wasn't far to the end now.

It was only that promise and the thought that if something serious did go wrong down there that it would take days to get anyone out, which forced me towards that impossible looking hole. Once inside it was so tight that with each push forward, you had to adjust the positioning of the battery, so it wouldn't get hooked and leave you stuck. In retrospect the idea of us going through in one long queue was perhaps unwise. It was tight enough as it was, waiting for the shoes in front of your face to move before you took your next slither made it feel quite a bit more frightening. And narrow as the tunnel was, it was also long, about fifty feet, which under the claustrophobic circumstances felt like it could have been a mile.

When we emerged out of the other end, others in our party were already on the final leg. We had been under for over five hours now. All that remained was a vertical tunnel - straight up, smooth walls, nothing to grip. It was a case of using the bridging technique we had employed to get over the first open gap, except instead of sliding horizontally, we needed to make little upward leaps, then quickly create the tension in our bodies between the walls in order to not fall straight back down again.

I made three attempts and failed. I was spent. I just didn't seem to have the strength to make it. I was about to give-up on the fourth attempt when I felt a hand stop me and push me up. It was The Dood come to my rescue. I managed to continue on my own and wait to haul The Dood up for his last few feet. We were in a small open space at the end of which we could see tiny rays of light filtering through bushes. We scrambled up over loose earth then burst through the opening.

We were barely free before we both turned and fell backwards into long grass. Our overalls were in tatters, our shoes were falling to pieces, and The Dood's simply disintegrated. But we were free. We looked up into the most beautiful blue sky either of us had ever seen, breathing air with thought purer than Everest's. We almost gripped the earth, making sure it was steady, and there, and not about to fall away beneath us. It wasn't as much fun as we'd hoped, but we had survived.

It's the aftermath of this story that usually gets the laughs, though we didn't find it funny. Once we got back to the clubhouse, and without saying a word to each other or anyone else, the two of us got in our separate cars and headed home. Once we reached a town about half-way there, The Dood pulled over and I did likewise. We went into a café and ordered some well-earned food, just pointing to the menu. Not a word was spoken. When we finished we both threw in our share and walked back to our cars. An hour and a half later we were back home, had showers, and went to our respective beds. Gary and Jan didn't get home until later, which saved us from having to explain it all.

For two whole weeks The Dood spoke to no one. He still hasn't ever said anything to anyone about it. Me, I told the necessary, but it was some time before I could pick-up anything that fell under my desk. I will never, ever go caving again. Not even if there is a pretty girl with a torch.

I'm ready

I'm ready now it seems. Yesterday was my last scheduled session with my psychologist. From now on it will be on an as-need basis. We had a good chat about where I'm at and what the future holds. It all looks good. We'd almost finished when I stopped and said, "You know I had the weirdest dream before I came today."

I had fallen asleep during the middle of the day because of these new drugs I'm on, which is a rarity for me now. "I dreamed that I was surfing through this small, messy barrel which suddenly opened out into a bigger, cleaner barrel. It felt great. But then the barrel got bigger and bigger, until I thought, "Shit! this thing's way too big for me." And that's when the weirdest thing happened. Everything went deadly still. I was still in a barrel, but the water below was perfectly flat, with the wave curling over to make a sort of cave.

"Then my perspective changed. I turned ninety degrees to look back at the horizon. There was a distinct line between the flat water and the curling wave above. And then I started to move towards it. Now I was both afraid and curious. I moved with a sort of pulsing movement, until I passed through the horizon and everything turned black, a real nothingness black. The only thing that gave this new space any proportion was the sound of a type of music – what has been described as 'The Movement of the Spheres', or the sound of the universe turning. "This is death," I thought. I wasn't afraid, there was little to be curious about, my attention was simply tuned to the music. There was peace.

"And that's when I woke up and realized I had just half an hour to get to my session." Justine asked, "And what do you think your dream means?" I hadn't thought about it, I hadn't had time. But automatically the words came, "It means that one part of my life has died and I'm now ready to start a new life." We both just laughed.

www.ingramcontent.com/pod-product-compliance
Lightning Source LLC
Chambersburg PA
CBHW021159010426
R18062100001B/R180621PG41931CBX00041B/75